D1562842

Irish Women Speak

Clonakilty women of the 20th Century.

First Edition

Stories gathered by Alison Wickham to celebrate 400 years of Clonakilty's history as a town.

This book includes 15 stories from Women Speak.
Life for Clonakilty Women in the 1900's",
published in 2013.

With thanks for support from Cork County Council &
Creative Ireland, Co. Cork Grant Scheme.

Clár Éire Ildánach
Creative Ireland
Programme
2017–2022

Cork
County Council
Comhairle Contae Chorcaí

First published: September 2017 by Wickham Books

Published by:

Wickham Books
3 Old Chapel Lane
Clonakilty
County Cork
Ireland
Preferred contact: abwickham@gmail.com
ISBN: 978-0-9926815-2-4

Cover Design: Sara Haggerty
Photography: A Wickham

Contents

Ardfield Page 185

Location

Clonakilty area

Introduction

Three things motivated me to gather these stories and publish this book:

1. I wanted to give something tangible back to the town I have grown to love.
2. The two of us live comfortably in a renovated 700 square foot, two rooms up and two down, house where seven children were raised. *"How did they manage?"*
3. Little was documented of the everyday lives of ordinary Irish women and girls.

I published my first small effort in 2013. In 20th Century Ireland women had a great deal of hard physical work to raise a large family and ensure their needs were met, cope with political and economic realities, as well as support the man of the house. I also wanted to acknowledge the huge contributions to society at large, that these women made in the course of their role.

This collection of stories includes those from my first book. In total, they come from more than 36 Irish women from around 30 years of age to their mid 90's, who spent at least fifteen years of their lives in, or within 15km of Clonakilty, County Cork, Ireland. Clonakilty is a small town sited at the head of a large tidal bay on the rugged West Cork coastline, about one hours travel west from the city of Cork. The town is home to about 5,000 people in 2017 and its boundaries are formed by lush farmland and the Atlantic Ocean.

These accounts, unless otherwise noted, are from women who spoke to me personally, or generously gave their words in unpublished form. In a few cases, where women were no longer alive, close relatives drew from their own memory banks of mothers' and grandmothers' actions and stories. They contain a diversity of experiences that illustrate the many and different aspects of women's' lives in the 1900's, rather than complete biographies.

I thank all my remarkable sources for their great generosity in sharing their lives with me and in particular to the superb handwritten contribution of Margaret Feen, entitled Journey into Another Life: Growing up in West Cork in the 1920's, which gave me an enormous boost.

Thanks also to those who encouraged me in my project, in particular Dr Claudia Kinmonth for her Foreword and Geraldine Cullinane, who helped with promotion, and those who assisted with Irish translations and proof reading. Special thanks go to Geraldine O'Sullivan for the lovely artwork on the cover, and to Sara Haggerty for the cover design and other useful tips. Many of the photographs are not able to be credited due to the years that have elapsed. Photos of old photographs and other scenes are my own. Thanks are also due to my dear technology advisor, for his patience and support.

Any profits from the sale of this volume, will be donated to a project to further preserve and honour the lives of local women. On consideration, I plan to do this through encouragement of the recording of womens' stories and to facilitate publication of them via establishing a womens' history writing competition to be known as The Women Speak Awards. Further details will be forthcoming.

Foreword by Dr Claudia Kinmonth

On meeting Alison Wickham, at the launch of her first book in 2013, I had an immediate affinity for her and the importance of her work. I moved to West Cork, about the same time she did, soon after the publication of my first book, <u>Irish Country Furniture 1700-1950</u> (Yale University Press, 1993). Wickham moved to Clonakilty from New Zealand, and has also lived in America. My second book <u>Irish Rural Interiors in Art</u> (Yale, 2006), assembled hundreds of images of the insides of Irish farmhouses and cabins, the majority drawn by artists visiting Ireland from abroad, juxtaposed with early texts.

The most vivid images from diaries and travel journals survived from outsiders, whose viewpoints seemed sharpened by the contrast with their native cultures, rather than by the Irish, whose observations were perhaps dulled by familiarity.

By the 1950's about half the population was still cooking over an open hearth, and rural electrification was just beginning. The farm kitchen was the woman's workshop. The 'woman of the house' (or *bean an tí*) rose before her family, rekindled the fire, cooked, washed, cleaned, raised quantities of children and cared for small animals indoors, as well as tending to the needs of the men. Indoors cottage industries such as spinning, weaving, lace making, sewing and knitting augmented the household's income. On the smallest holdings, women (seldom ever men) raised poultry, and the money from eggs, feathers and flesh often exceeded the income their husbands raised from stock. The hen coop dresser, with kitchenware proudly displayed over rows of slatted straw-lined coops, enabled henwives to sustain egg production through the normally barren winter months. Most learnt to manage the fowl minutely, even knowing which hen had laid 'the cherished egg' before letting her out to forage.

The latter sort of information, from the 1930's archives of the Irish Folklore Commission, can be set against local stories from Clonakilty, such as that of the farmer's daughter, who recalled her mother keeping guinea fowl, which needed special care from the children, as they tended to roost in trees. Such small enterprises were so numerous that a lorry came to Clonakilty each week, to buy hens and eggs, and take them to Cork. One girl and her sister walked two miles to visit their grandmother, accompanied by two pet hens 'which liked to walk with them'. They were also tasked with loading the hen turkey into the family pram, at mating time to take it to the neighbour's farm, yet the girls were sheltered from any mating process.

An outsider settling in Clonakilty in the 1960's, was surprised to observe women still labouriously carrying water in buckets from rainwater barrels, or the pump in the street. The weekly routine was often dictated by specific days dedicated to basic tasks. Wash day was especially loathed, involving not only carrying the buckets, but soaking, soaping the clothes on the table top, rinsing, wringing and then hanging things out to dry. Ironing was done on another day, then housework (including cleaning windows), baking, and bicycling to town for provisions on another. One girl growing up on the coastal headland of Barryroe. recalls how 'farming was considered "men's work" and we women and girls were concerned mainly with the house'. So she was never able to discover how many cattle they owned, or the farm's acreage. It was left to the women to scrub and rinse the six milk churns by hand with Vim abrasive powder (and no gloves), until the bulk milk tank was installed. Other contrasts between how the men and women were treated emerge during accounts of wakes, when the women drank tea and the menfolk liquor. The women sat near the coffin, while the men were in the parlour. The tradition of holding the Stations, is one that still survives locally. The special food prepared for this event included 'laden tiered cake-stands with slices of porter cake and buns of all descriptions' and mother's white soda cakes 'she shaped in a round and marked with a cross and a dimple in the centre of each quarter', or the rarely purchased sliced pan bought from Houlihan's who 'wrapped it especially for you in crisp white paper'.

The story provided by a traveller woman describes the 'bartering of flowers, clothes pegs, safety pins, combs or camphor balls, for butter, sugar and eggs for our children'. She explains how the tradition of burning the caravan after the death of a resident, not only freed the spirit but 'brought peace to the families, as there was no fighting over the loved one's possessions'.

The stories gathered here span the spectrum of Clonakilty life. In contrast, one far more fortunate girl, had a job as a wages clerk for a company in Cork. She was well paid, but it left her unprepared as a new wife at which point she 'didn't know how to boil an egg'. Repeatedly we read of girls who at age 13 or 14, were propelled into adulthood prematurely, as they left school to take over the role of running the household, when their mothers fell ill.

The women's stories sensitively gleaned by Wickham include many more similarly detailed accounts, which are akin to gold dust to the historian, yet make fascinating reading for those familiar or unfamiliar with Irish rural culture. Those from the older women are especially revealing, as their memories reach back to times that now seem astonishingly primitive and different, in today's Internet dominated world. A sense of contrast emerges within many narratives. The late Margaret Feen's brilliantly detailed story recalls how the Irish woman's role in the 1920's was 'only a degree above slavery' when men 'ruled over their women with a rod of iron'.

Wickham's saving of such rare descriptions is enriched by her sense of appreciation, as an outsider looking in. Her book assembles accounts from people whose voices might never otherwise have been preserved, and whose stories are a highly valuable addition to the minority of historical publications that explore the role of women, rather than men.

Claudia Kinmonth PhD MA(RCA) BTecHND
Visiting Research Fellow, National University of Ireland, Galway

P. Beechinor

My childhood was very nice as we had a lot of company coming and going to our home. My parents were farmers and we sold milk to the local villagers who came twice a day to collect it bringing their own jugs or sweet tins to be filled. They always sat down for a chat, especially in the evening. The charge at the time was two pence a pint but sometimes it varied up or down by a halfpenny. A 'sup for the cat' was always added free. There was no electricity in the area in the 1930's and 40's so refrigeration was not available to us. There was very little radio, some homes had battery-operated sets but as we didn't have one we depended on reading. The Cork Weekly Examiner, published on a Thursday, and Southern Star, published on Friday, was the means of our general news. Things would happen and you wouldn't know about them for a few days. The main source of information was the men's daily meeting at the creamery when they delivered the milk in churns. Our house was known as a scoraiochting house. This was a very old Irish custom where neighbours would gather at night to exchange news, stories of local interest and folklore and we played cards or rings[1].

I remember the effects on neutral Ireland of World War Two. There was rationing of tea, sugar and other items. Ration books were distributed to every person and one had to have coupons for such goods, especially clothes. When a person went to buy an item of clothing there was a price plus the number of coupons required and you had to have the correct number of coupons, or it was impossible to purchase. Woodbine cigarettes were very scarce and they

---

[1] A game like darts where hard rubber rings would be aimed at some 12 pegs set into a board on a wall. It cost a penny to participate, and this would fund the prize.

were sold singly so as to distribute them as evenly as possible. We had two farm workers and they and my father had their own rations of sugar placed by my mother into three jam pots, each marked with their own name and that had to last them the week. The government issued a grant for jam sugar, which we used for raspberry and loganberry jam making. There was an inspection to ensure that pots of jam resulted from the special allowance. A train robbery also occurred in the locality during the war. Tea and other rationed goods destined for the grocery shops were stolen, never recovered and no culprit was ever found for this crime.

At that time Sunday was a day of rest and no work would be done except for what was absolutely necessary. My father would have been working in the fields with horses all the week and after Mass on Sunday would rest on the settle[2] in the kitchen. My mother would have done all the necessaries for Sunday on the Saturday. Sometimes we would visit near relations, travelling by pony and trap, or family would visit us using the same mode of transport.

Our village had its own Local Defence Force (LDF) volunteers who used to train and march in the early evening about 7pm. I was the eldest of three children and one Sunday afternoon in the 1940's we were playing in the farmyard when we were startled to see strange uniformed soldiers with weapons marching across the fields. We ran to call our mother and brought her to see what was happening. However, by then they had all gone into hiding and she thought we were imagining it and went back into the house. We then crossed the main road outside our house where there was a stream and looked over the bridge: to our horror there they were again! Soldiers with weapons, who told us to get away and not come back! We

[2] Seat which could convert to a bed

were then convinced that war had come to Ireland. Mother was called again and went out to them to be told it was a big military manoeuvre in our village. All the LDF volunteers from all over West Cork were taking part. A flag on a flagpole in the centre of the village was the target for the Irish Army to capture from the LDF who were guarding it. The Army had a large number of artillery gun carriages, other artillery that we had never seen before, as well as lorry loads of soldiers that all paraded on the roads around the village. We children were very frightened and really convinced that war had come! The next day we were surprised that the Army had captured the flag and beat the LDF.

Most of the food we ate was produced on our land. About twice a year a pig would be killed and most of the meat salted and preserved in a wooden barrel. Each neighbour would be a given a pork roast . When they killed their own pig they would reciprocate. The blood and intestines were collected for black puddings. I went to the river with mother to rinse the intestines because the forceful flow of the water cleaned them really well. We took them home and washed them again in spring water. Mother mixed the congealed blood together with oatmeal, onions and seasonings. Then she tied off one end of the intestines and stuffed them with a spoon. Then they would be boiled until cooked. The sliced black puddings were served fried like bacon rashers. The home-killed salted pork was served after boiling too and was always paler in colour than that seen in the shops today. We grew our own carrots, turnips, cabbages and potatoes. Dinner was at 1pm and we had an egg and brown bread for breakfast and supper. Stewed apple was also often on the menu. The cooking was done on a range that burned coal, timber or peat.

My mother kept hens and raised 100 turkeys each year too. Every Friday a lorry from Cork stopped in the villages along the way, and in Clonakilty, to buy hens and eggs to take back to Cork. For a while mother also kept Guinea hens for eggs and hatching. They roamed free but had to be shut up early at night or else they would fly into the trees to roost. I used to watch them at a distance along a fence for long periods to discover the location of the nest. I put a glove on my hand to remove the egg as soon as it was laid, to avoid it being rejected by the broody hen. The eggs for hatching sold at two shillings and sixpence a dozen. My mother worked hard and the income her work created helped us a lot. Mother cycled into Clonakilty for her shopping.

Primary school lasted until seventh class. At age about 14 years I came to town for secondary school by bicycle for two years. Then my father died and I was needed to help my mother on the farm. We milked the cows by hand together, along with another man to help. In my father's time our farm also grew linen flax, but it was a very labour intensive and difficult job.

We had a pony and trap for transport in the early days. Just after the Second World War ended, my first car journey took place when we hired one to bring my mother home from hospital. The comfort of the small Ford far exceeded that of the pony and trap. I have also never forgotten the thrill of my first bus trip to Cork. My mother, neighbour and I were visiting a sick neighbour in the Bon Secours in Cork. I was so excited by the speed and scenery as the trees and farmland flashed before my eyes.

Diversions outside home were not that frequent. Sometimes we went by train to the Courtmacsherry regatta and we followed the trotting horses in the village at Little

Christmas[3]. More frequently there were old time dances in the village and the occasional platform dancing where someone played an accordion to provide the music. Afterwards there would be a collection to pay the musician. Meeting at a dance was a common way of finding a husband as women were not then welcome in pubs and there were few other ways of meeting someone. Occasionally a matchmaker arranged marriages.

In those times children and young people were protected from a lot of information about life. If we children were sent to the pub to buy from a limited range of groceries they carried, we were always sent to the kitchen door never to the bar. When I asked my mother where our new baby came from, she said, "The nurse delivered the baby to me in the basket of her bicycle, and I was dead happy". "Found amongst the cabbages", was another description in use.

Electricity came to the locality in 1950 and it changed and modernised everything and made life easier. A milk plant opened in our nearest town selling pasteurised milk. The government bought in new regulations for selling milk so that was the end of milk sales for us, but a few villagers kept calling but not as regular. There was a small privately owned hall in the village that was rented to any users. It was a galvanised iron structure that was the centre of socialising during the winter. Two lads from Bandon came once a week and showed black and white films, which were a great treat. An agricultural class was also held in this hall and the farmers' sons attended it. Later a branch of Macra Na Feirme arose from this. The Irish Countrywomen's Association formed a branch later and the whole scene changed for the better.

---

[3] January 6, also known as the Feast of the Epiphany and in Ireland: Women's Little Christmas" a traditional time of relaxation for women.

So ends one era, and begins another…

A group from Ballinascarthy ICA on a day out in the late 1950's.

Margaret and Katherine O'Leary

My married name is Margaret Duffy and I was born in 1906. I had two brothers and six sisters, Katherine being one year older than me. My family called me Madge and Katherine, Kitty. Our father was Arthur O'Leary and mother was born Mary Cooke. We grew up near Clonakilty. Killavarrig is where our farm was, and we children all helped out with the usual farm chores.

Left Katherine and right Margaret circa 1930.

At school in Timoleague we knew that some of the teachers looked down on those of us from farm families. We'd walk the four miles to school barefoot to save the leather on our shoes, and only put them on when we got to school. One time we passed the Argideen Vale Lawn Tennis and Croquet Club where the wealthy Protestants played tennis. Naturally, we were curious about what happened there and we peeked in. We were shooed away by the caretaker, clearly giving us the message it wasn't a place for people like us.

We spent six days a week walking, five to school, and one to church. Kitty, my older sister, might have told you that when we were out walking, if we ran into the priest's dog, we would all run and hide in the bushes. For the priestwouldn't be far behind and if he found us, he would ask us our Catechism, and if we didn't know it, he'd go and tell our mother who would give us a right spanking.

Our mother, God bless her soul, was strict and some of us children were more willing to push the boundaries than others. One time our mother asked us to fill up her containers with holy water at the well dedicated to the Blessed Virgin. It was half way to the church. Kitty said to our younger sister Bridy and me, "We're not going, we're going to the local well, and she won't know the difference!" Bridy and I were scared, but we followed Kitty, taking extra time as if we'd gone all the way to Lady's Well. When we got back, we were each too scared to tell, since the other two would have gotten in trouble. And there was our poor dear mother; going round the house, blessing everything with local well water, thinking it was holy water.

Kitty, being older, was the brave one who could tell the stories and make us all laugh. She wasn't as interested in school, but I just loved it. They had brought Irish back as a subject, and oh how difficult that was; I didn't care for it at all. Still, my marks were good and I managed to go on to Secondary Top classes at the Convent of Mercy. We learned French there, the way they taught that, it was so much easier than Irish!

Life was simple as we weren't a family of much means. It was not like today, buying whatever you like at the grocery store. On the way to school, we used to pass an apple orchard. When the apples were in season, what I wouldn't have done for a bite of one. The others would sneak in and steal a few. I wouldn't be caught stealing, but what else could I do but protect the others from being caught? I was their lookout. Fruit was indeed a luxury, so much so, that getting an orange for Christmas was a big treat.

On Sundays we would have to go to Mass in shifts, as we didn't have enough hats for all the girls to wear. When the first shift were walking back home, we'd meet our sisters on the way to the church, and they'd give us the hats so we could go to mass with our heads covered, as was the way then.

Sure, we didn't feel we were lacking. Our house was something of a meeting ground for music and dances on Saturday evenings. Lawrence, my older brother, would play the fiddle. When the weather was fair, we'd have the gatherings just outside the house. It was a gay time, but not without the pull of the times. The Royal Irish Constabulary[4] took in my brother Arthur for questioning on suspicion he'd hid armaments on our land during the Civil War. There was no evidence, so they let him go. He never would tell us if he had or hadn't. Our family was against dividing Ireland and allowing it to still be partially under the British Empire.

As the tide turned in favour of those supporting the treaty, it became clear to me that perhaps job prospects might be limited for a daughter from a family of the losing side. Not to mention that my parents simply didn't have the means to send me on to teacher training. So I left my dream of becoming a teacher behind and set off for America when I was about nineteen. Kitty had gone the year before at eighteen, to a job as a household helper, with some help from my mother's sister who was working

---

[4] Following the Civil War the Garda Síochána na hÉireann were established, with a new name on 8 August 1923.

there. Kitty was very homesick and with her encouragement and help from our aunt, they managed to support me to go as well.

What a journey it had been from our home in Killavarrig. It wasn't just the days-long journey on that ship from Queenstown[5], where I felt I would die in those windowless, below sea level cabins. If only I had thought of going up to the decks, maybe I wouldn't have been so ill. Ah no, I wouldn't have dreamed that we'd be allowed up there.

Kitty had found work in Massachusetts. When I arrived in New York, a cousin met me and took me on the subway to where we would stay before I headed to Boston. There on the subway I saw, for the first time in my life, a black man. I couldn't stop staring until my cousin nudged me to stop being so rude.

I worked for 12 years in Milton[6], Massachusetts for the Walcott family. They were good to me: I had my own room. What a luxury that was after sharing a bed with four of my sisters for so long. My main jobs included setting the table and serving the dinners. I was always very particular about these things, long after I left the job. I had other things to do as well, and sometimes, after Mrs Walcott noticed I was well able, I would help her daughter with her homework.

When Kitty and I went back to Ireland in 1932 for the Eucharistic Congress in Dublin[7], before I had met my husband, what a scandal! We had cut our hair into bobs and we wore slacks! No women in rural Ireland then wore short hair and they were all still wearing skirts. After meeting our family at home, we went in two carloads up to Dublin for the Congress. It was good to be home, but

---

[5] Now known as Cobh
[6] An affluent suburb of Boston.
[7] International gathering of hierarchy & laity of the Roman Catholic Church.

sadly we knew it wouldn't be our home anymore. Even Dad knew, and before we took the ship back to America, he told us it would be the last time he saw us, and it was.

When I returned to the Walcotts I'd look out the window from my work and see Charles Duffy in his police uniform, patrolling the neighbourhood. Somehow, we got to chatting. Nothing like a man in uniform, that's what I told my granddaughter once and isn't it the truth? What a good man he was, God rest his soul. When we married, the Walcotts gave me a set of china.

Coming to America and marrying Charles, my life was nothing like Killavarrig times. His parents had emigrated from Donegal, and for him growing up without the life of music around him, he couldn't bear hearing Irish music. It was only with my granddaughters that I could get up for a bit of a jig in the sitting room, or even by the record player in the dining room when the table was folded up.

It wasn't until 1965, just before my son Charlie was getting married, that I took a plane for the first time in my life and flew back to Ireland. Kitty and I went together and stayed with our sister Annie on Pearse Street. We had a great time and even went to Killarney. But still, it was sad to see everyone 30 years older than when I'd last seen them. I never went back.

My son Charlie took his wife Ivy to Ireland when they were expecting their first child. They met Lawrence and his wife Nora, Arthur and some of my other sisters who still lived in the area. It's grand that they did the trip and had two beautiful daughters who both have visited Ireland. One of them, Tara, has moved to the west coast of Ireland and has her own small child now growing up on the lands that held no future for us in the 1920s. She has visited Clonakilty, seen where the farm was, and met her cousins there too. One of my nieces is a retired primary school teacher, fluent in Irish! My great grand-daughter, oh how I would have loved to meet her. I hear she likes Gaelige and has even gone to tennis camp in Galway city. And my great-niece, she went on to win several cups at the very same club in Timoleague that shooed me away. Would you believe it? The places you go, jobs you can have, people have everything now. God bless you.

Margaret Duffy passed away in 1995.

As told in Margaret's voice, by her grand-daughter Tara Duffy, in consultation with Margaret's son Charlie, and other family members.

****

Frances Harrington

Uneventful, would be a word I would use to describe my life and the happiest days were those spent with my birth family and then my own family. I was born in 1921 in my parent's home in Clonakilty with the local doctor in attendance. He lived just two doors away. There was only one doctor in the town at that time: a very approachable, hard-working man out night and day, who sadly lived a short life.

We lived in a large, comfortable house on the main street. This was unusual in two respects; an extension to the house was a grocery store and a coal yard managed by an uncle, so our home had no garden at all: the yard was used for the horses and carts of customers. Secondly, my father was a farmer. My mother frequently said, "I brought up seven children on the side of the street in Clonakilty, but we had acres just a mile down the road."

My birth family included an older brother, two younger brothers, and two younger twin sisters. The youngest boy died at eighteen months of meningitis, which was prevalent at that time. I did not need to be a help to my mother as we had a country girl, who lived in. She started each day at 6am and kept the coal range going and cooked the meals for the family. She also did the majority of the laundry, most of which was done by hand in a large wooden tub. Items like towels were boiled and the special occasion tablecloths sent to the local laundry. Laundry was dried on lines in the yard out back. A second girl was employed to look after the twins. They were wheeled about in a double pram. It was not easy to manage on Clonakilty's narrow footpaths; I discovered this for myself when taking them for a walk.

I began my schooling at the age of five at the local convent. A very wrinkled old nun greeted us when we arrived, and so frightened me that I caused quite a stir. However, I settled into school life and recall enjoying drawing, playing with Plasticine and energetic games of tig tag. Being the niece of the Monsignor was not always easy, and I vividly remember the humiliation I suffered when I was made an example of by a vindictive nun in front of my uncle, for missing my catechism. A sharp caning across the hands was also something that occurred rather more frequently than I would have liked.

My mother did not approve of us playing in the street or crossroads dancing, but we did have a simple little two-room place at Inchydoney where we could stay. It was hard to sleep, as it was often too noisy from the wind. Sometimes we travelled there by pony and trap just to take tea and swim in our modest bathing costumes. There was little there then, apart from a big country house hotel.

In those days, confirmations only happened once every three or four years when the Bishop and his man came down from Cork. In my family we received bicycles for our confirmation, which gave us great mobility. My mother came from Bandon and we went there frequently for holidays by pony and trap, as there was no convenient route between Clonakilty and her family home by train.

As there was no girl's secondary school in Clonakilty, I went to live with my mother's sister in Cork and attended the Ursuline Convent Secondary School on Patricks Hill. They were happy times there in a family with girls my age. I enjoyed playing hockey. It was not available in Clonakilty because there was a prejudice against English games and camogie, the GAA girls' game, was rather rough. At 17 and a half years old I left secondary education, having not been pressed to do the matriculation exam. My mother thought it a good idea that I should go to cookery school at the

Edinburgh College of Domestic Science, studying household management and high-class cookery. Another girl, who was a distant relative from Crookstown, travelled there with me. Together we boarded in the School for Catering. After I had completed the course my brothers said, 'What are you doing over there now there is a war on?' They encouraged me to return home.

At Easter in 1942 I married at the age of 21, an uncommonly young age for a girl then. My husband was a Skibbereen man in his early thirties who practised law and we met in Clonakilty, where he had an office in town. (Pubs were not places for women to meet people then. The only time it was decent was after funerals, when a discreet glass of sherry might be sipped in the seclusion of the 'snug' or private bar.)

We travelled up to Cork to choose the engagement ring together and had the distinction of the first white wedding[8] in the Clonakilty church. My uncle, the Monsignor officiated with my two sisters as brides-maids. The hotel at Inchydoney Island was the setting for our wedding breakfast, which we reached by car. Wartime ruled out a honeymoon in mainland Europe so we went to Dublin.

My husband was a good man who recognised how the legal system and the church kept women in Ireland down. He insisted that both our names should be on our legal ownership papers, not just the man's name as was customary. Women did not have chequebooks and most were reliant on housekeeping money doled out by their husband.

After our marriage we lived in town at Astna Square in a house with a rented shop below and accommodation over. There was no backyard or land with it, so as our family grew to three children we moved out onto the

---

[8] A fashion begun by Queen Victoria.

Island Road. We had a big house with views of the bay, a vegetable garden and our own Jersey cow. I had household help but made butter for our own use and sold surplus to the local shops. We grew the things we could not buy from the store, e.g. peas, French beans, leeks, as well as having chickens. The house had tap water indoors but it had to be hand pumped from our own well, as there was no electrification until the 1950's. Meals were cooked on the range but as coal was rationed, turf (often still wet) and timber, cut by my husband, were the main fuels available.

For entertainment lady friends would gather in ones or two's at 'At Homes'. We made sponge cakes from our own eggs and bought special white flour for them. Apple tart or apple cakes were also popular. Occasionally travelling players came to Clonakilty and there was also an active cinema. About once a week I walked from Youghals to Kilgarriffe to see my relations.

During World War 2 there were shortages of food like raisins, bananas and oranges along with white flour. My uncle's shop had to declare what foods were rationed, these included tea and sugar and even baby had a share. Irel coffee essence became the popular substitute for coffee. During this period we bought our clothing in Cork but my mother also made clothes on a hand operated sewing machine. When electrification finally arrived it was wonderful to no longer need the fragile and expensive Tilley lamps, which needed such care to move from room to room.

Our daughters went away to board at secondary school in Cork and our son to Holy Ghost in Dublin. After my eldest brother died my father and mother moved out to a house on The Miles. My mother, who lived to be 104, frequently cycled from there to see me at Youghals. Later she had an old Ford car, which she drove without making much use of the gears. As the car rattled complaining up our drive, my son used to amuse us by saying, "Here comes the agony".

****

A beautiful old hearth with cooking equipment at the Michael Collins Centre, Castleview, Clonakilty.

Child of the 1940's

Money was tight when we were children. We went to stay with more affluent relations in the summer, and they sent us back with their unwanted woollen coats. These would be taken to a dressmaker in Clonakilty who turned them. In other words, remade them by putting the old outside on the inside. I was the last to get the big symbols of maturity then, nylons[9] and Cuban heels.

There was one very strict nun in the convent secondary school. If she deemed our knee-length skirts too short she would pin newspapers around the hem, which the unlucky girl had to wear for the day. Modesty was everything and to get pregnant was the biggest shame a girl could bring upon her family. She also told us, 'Even if a sperm lands on your knee, it can crawl up and get you pregnant'. The Catholic Church was totally in control of our lives. Its influence extended from the church to the schools and the health care system.

At home laundry was still done by hand in a wooden tub with a washboard and food was kept in a food safe. This was a small cupboard outside of the house with mesh on the sides to let the breeze travel through. It provided a cool, vermin free place to store meat and other perishables for short periods.

There were only about four streetlights in town at the time. A wallpaper factory was a major employer. Many Clonakilty people embraced the trend of wallpaper from the local factory on the walls of their homes. The more grand homes of the senior factory staff had quite an

---

[9] Nylon stockings reached to above the knee and were held in place by clips hanging from suspender belts, or by twisting the stocking tops and tucking the twist in

influence on the local's pride in their own dwellings and their aspirations.

A cinema provided entertainment. It had a very long bench at the back where the courting couples used to sit. Lots of kissing went on there in that chaste era.

When I finished school I took up one of the few options allowing girls to move away from home and trained as a nurse. In the 1960's, when I was qualified and working on night shift, I saw my first condom. When patients were admitted via A & E their pockets were emptied and the contents checked and put in safe keeping. A condom had been found this way and it was sent the rounds of some of the nurses on night duty. What a talking point it provided as no one had seen one before, as contraception was not available in Ireland until the 1980's.

A food safe.

Sisters of the Clonakilty Diaspora

My mum Theresa Burke lived in Clonakilty at Fachtna Bridge and then Assumption Place from her birth in 1930 until she moved to England around 1961. I remember visiting her parents' home in Assumption Place with her, when I was a child. Climbing the many steep steps to the front door, the steeply angled garden at the back, then crossing a little lane to a field where a cow grazed, a novelty for us London city kids.

Family history has it that her father ran off to Dublin and fought in the Easter Rising, aged about 15. We understand he lied about his date of birth in order to enlist. He was in prison in England afterwards. The family felt the shame of this prison stay, but it was unavoidable because that was what the British did to their captives. They broke them up to avoid further rebellions and put them in prisons in various places. He eventually went back and settled in Clonakilty, where he made his living by fixing things like clocks, watches, boat and car engines. My mum said he was unsettled all his life and never made enough money. Her mother supplemented their diet by raising a flock of hens. Every year she would go and buy a batch of 12 chicks. Mum said she loved her hens and took great pleasure from them.

Life never sounded easy or particularly happy for Mum's family growing up. This makes more sense to me now that I've read some of the archive material that was published in 2016 about the War of Independence. Experiences were still raw for the participants and it was very hard to come back and resume normal life after living through the fighting and all that they had seen. It seems he was never an affectionate father and very strict with the children. My mum recalls that her father got a pension later, but we haven't been able to find him in the 1916 archives, due to other men having identical personal details. One thing I have always wondered about was how my mother and her siblings grew up believing in the new Irish state to their core. Yet at the same time, they were dominated by the church - expected to take the priest's view on all manner of stuff. How does that all add up?

My mother became a strong and resourceful woman. She was the eldest of four children; two girls and two boys who all walked to school in the town. The nuns weren't very nice to their pupils. My mother told us that there were very poor country girls who would walk miles to school and for sustenance, eat berries along the way. The nuns were cruel about the state of their clothes and shoes. Back then the town girls were viewed as superior to the country ones, which was so unfair. The nuns were quite authoritarian and decided what the girl's careers should be. Mum was sent to the Clonakilty Technical School at 15 to be trained as a short-hand typist. She became very skilled and fast. Her sister Margaret was sent at 16 years of age to Braintree in England, to train as a nurse. It was there that Margaret met her American husband to be.

I'm not sure how old Mum was, maybe 18, when she got a job working for the Cork County Council in offices near the Clonakilty Hospital , in the department that looked after health services. She continued working there until she was about 30. She travelled about with a doctor keeping records of childhood immunisation including for polio. There was a polio epidemic in Cork in 1956 and the following year immunisation was introduced. She remembers the rural electrification scheme being implemented in the early 1950's and empty cottages being sold with an acre of land for £10. As young working women, they had no interest in country cottages so turned their noses up at the idea of purchasing one, a decision that she regretted later in life. Her boss in the council was a woman called Miss Cotter, who was very brave when young. As a teen she had carried messages in the Civil War and was known as the Bantry Carrier Pigeon. She could cycle past the soldiers with messages as it would never occur to them to question a young girl.

Mum often spoke about the fantastic evening classes in Clonakilty and how all the young people, male and female, went to them. It was something to do on winter evenings. She learned many skills which I remember her applying throughout my childhood; dressmaking, basket weaving, wallpapering. She was most interested in the arts and crafts type things. I remember her buying a sheep's fleece and curing it herself to make mittens and a rug. She terrified us by using a blow torch to strip paint off the doors in the house they eventually bought in London. Knitting was also a favourite hobby.

Mum met our father at a dance; they were a very striking couple. In 1960 she married in London making a beautiful bride in her just below knee length white gown with her sister and friend wearing similar very fashionable bridesmaid dresses, in attendance.

In 1964 Mum was living in Clonakilty taking care of her mother who was dying of leukaemia. Mum was expecting a baby and I was delivered in the Bandon Hospital. My dad (from Skibbereen) was in London with all the other young Irish men trying to get a start financially. My mother emigrated to London to join my dad, after her mother died in the mid 1960's.

I imagine it was because their mother had just passed away that we went first to Germany to stay with her sister, Margaret, who was married to an American Air Force man. I believe we spent about six months with them. I learned to walk and talk with my cousins on the American base so my first accent was American! Over the course of about a decade my Aunt Margaret and her husband went on to live in various US Air Force bases in Europe where she gave birth to four children before going to San Diego to live when her children were teenagers. Later my aunt Margaret divorced her husband and made her own way as a nurse in San Diego. She remarried and had a very happy life in California.

Mum and Dad got a start together in London by agreeing to be caretakers of a huge rooming house in Belsize Square in Hampstead. I think the rent was cheaper because they did maintenance and collected rents. Life there is my first childhood memory. The house contained about 12 bedsitting rooms and we lived in two rooms on the ground floor. My brother and I shared the bedroom and my parents slept in the big room that also served as living room and kitchen. My parents viewed living in London as a great experience and opportunity. They were not sentimental about Ireland at all and did not belong to the nostalgic clubs. Their membership of the Catholic Church kept them in touch with their Irish friends and we children went to the local Catholic Schools. We were very happy there, where a majority of children were also Irish. It was a very positive experience for me and I received an excellent education amongst the liberal Sacred Heart nuns, who were early adopters of ordinary dress and broadened our outlooks on so many important and international things.

There were a few amusing incidents as we first settled in. My mother could not find "brack" to buy in any bakery. She did not realise at first that "brack"is not a universally known word for bread containing dried fruit. At nine or ten years old I used to be embarrassed at my mother's Irish friendliness in talking to everyone wherever she went, so different to the cool reserve of the British. I have a distinct memory of Mum's cousins Annie and Francie from Glandore coming to visit us in London. We were all going somewhere on the tube and Annie, was moving too slowly and got carried on to the next station. We all had to jump back on the next train and go on to the next station to find her. No mobile phones in those days!

Mum did Parish work visiting elderly people and ended up being hired by Camden Council to do it. I guess it was a form of home help. She also trained as a Samaritan and later she used her administrative skills as a volunteer in a Catholic home for women with learning disabilities. She helped the nuns maintain the records, and visited socially with the women. She always went back to West Cork to visit but rarely to Clonakilty, as we no longer had family living there. Her father died in about 1973 and had an IRA funeral in Clonakilty. I remember the old men in black coats firing shots over his grave.

We visited Glandore and Toe Head every summer throughout my childhood and I am really grateful for the hinterland it gave me. I never felt confined to London.

****

Mrs K

Life in Clonakilty began for me in 1947 and I married one year later at 20 years old. My husband, a carpenter, and I lived in a lodge on the Island Road at first. In the early 1950's we moved into a two bedroom semi-detached house in a new social housing estate. Our house was a very simple one when we moved in, just two rooms up and two down. There was an iron cooker fired by coal and wood in the main downstairs room (which we strung lines in front of for drying clothes in wet weather) and a little pantry with a sink off the other room. Upstairs there were two rooms with the only bathroom facility being a toilet. Soon after moving in we installed an electric cooker and a bath. Over the years we added more rooms on to increase the convenience and comfort of the house. Nine children were born to us there.

By today's standards life was very hard but I believe we were happier then. The community was a close one and very safe and supportive. Crime did not seem to be a problem to worry about. People did their best with what they had to hand and saved for the things they needed. Religion and church attendance were an important part of life, giving much comfort and guidance.

Except for the cooker, household appliances did not exist. Our hands did all the work of meal preparation and mending and I did the laundry in the sink. After my husband met with an accident that disabled him, I had to support the family by working as a nurse's helper at Mount Carmel hospital. Many were the times that I was hanging the washing out to dry at two in the morning, after the end of my shift. I loved my work with the patients at the hospital, especially nursing the men. I also looked after the nuns at night by helping them. They were always trying to get me to take over the meals for the hospital, as they knew I could cook, but I was reluctant to leave the care of patients, because I loved it so much. However, one day a nun told me that God was calling me to do the cooking, and so I did.

I cooked for 50 or so patients with the help of another girl. We used a coal range to cook the food and sometimes it was necessary for us to get the coal ourselves if we didn't want the cooker to go out. Usually I arrived at work at about 7.30 am and together we prepared and cooked the breakfast of porridge, bread and tea. We then began preparations for the main meal of the day, dinner. This consisted of things like lovely ham or bacon with fresh vegetables. The floury potatoes were boiled in their skins and peeled by the patients themselves.

The nun who looked after the office served up the meals and the ward's maids carried these via the stairs to the patients, as there were no lifts in the hospital. The ward staff and nuns fed the less able patients first, at 12.30pm, and the rest of the patients had dinner at 1pm. In the afternoon my assistant and I could go back home for an hour or two. At 5.30pm a lighter tea was served, maybe a fry or a boiled egg, with bread and butter. Morning and afternoon tea consisted of tea or milk, with bread, biscuit or cake in the afternoon. We did all the cleaning up and washing of dishes by hand ourselves as there were no dishwashers. I usually got home by 6pm but sometimes it was later. I retired from this job at the age of 62 but continued to look after the elderly nuns several nights each week. In total it was for about 20 years. I would start work there at about 9 pm and finish at 6.30 am, catching up on my sleep during the day.

My older boys were a wonderful help to me when they were young. They took jobs in the town on holidays and weekends and contributed to the household budget. As they grew old enough my daughters were given jobs in the hospital in the school holidays. The nuns were very good to us. All my children are alive and well in Ireland. Five of them are nurses.

****

Dwellings erected by the local authority in the 1950's, some of the ones on the right have later additions at the back. Many are now privately owned.

Mary

Life began for me on a snowy February night in 1969. My mother rested happily in the Bandon Community Hospital knowing that, after six sons, the eldest aged 14; she had produced a daughter at last. Following her first three children my mother was unwell for four or five years and so there was a gap until the final four children were born. I was taken home to a two-story cottage in a local village. My father was a transporting locally grown sugar beet to the factory at Mallow. He was a hardworking and sociable person and en route he often gave people lifts into and out of Cork City. Thumbing a lift was a common way for people to travel about then.

My mother was so happy to have a girl about the house that she kept me at home until I was five and a half. Her health was unstable all throughout my youth. She had periods when she was well and others when she was not. We had happy times, when we worked together she would often say, "Let's sit down and have a chat in the garden for twenty minutes". We might be picking lettuce leaves or sitting with some other light work. She taught me that a fresh lettuce leaf and some bread and butter make the most delicious sandwich. When she was unwell, I did all the cooking and cleaning from an early age. Feeding the men was a big part of it. It was a very male household and in keeping with the times in which we lived, the mens' needs were always put first. We managed with the help of our Nana who lived just up the road from us. My three older brothers provided a lot for the home once they were working.

The visits from my mother's sisters in England were a big thing for us. They sometimes came on their holidays from nursing and hotel work and would stay with Nana.

There was always a lot of news to discuss and gifts. One time, knowing that I had only ever had hand-me-down toys, they brought me a red metal car that I could sit in and drive about using the foot pedals. How exciting it was for me!

On my first day walking to school, my brothers ran ahead of me and got there first. When I arrived, the schoolmaster's first words to me were, "Are you cold?" Then he said, "If you put out your hand a couple of slaps [with the ruler] will warm you up!" I was taken aback and didn't take up his offer. The narrow edge of the ruler was how they kept discipline then. Another punishment used at school was to make the girls walk around the school-yard holding hands with a boy, one who had also misbehaved. More serious punishment involved being taken to the Priest's house. The only time this happened to me for some silly thing I did, the Priest was not at home so I don't know what the punishment would have been. Probably it was mostly just the shame of it and letting your family down, which was something we all worried about a lot. Despite this, my infant schooldays were carefree and happy. In my year at school there were only four of us girls. As I was older than the other children when I began school, I decided myself to insist on taking my First Holy Communion at the age of seven, even though I was only in the High Infants Class. I was happy that I was allowed. School was very heavily influenced by the Catholic religion.

From the ages of thirteen to nineteen I attended Boarding School in Rosscarbery due to my mother's ill health. My 26-year-old brother paid my boarding school fees for the entire six years I was there, and for that I am appreciative. I was happy at boarding school, as it was the first time I had lived with other girls and I made life-long friendships. My girlfriends became the sisters I never had.

When I was 15 my father suffered a stroke just prior to Christmas. Despite being up and down to Cork Hospital he never regained his ability to speak or walk, and sadly passed away six months later. It was the end of an era for our family as we seldom all gathered together again in the years ahead.

Before I sat the Leaving Certificate I knew that I wanted to train as a nurse on completion of my schooling. It was something I had always wanted. It was very hard to get nurse training in Ireland at that time and we felt it was often more of a case of "who" you knew, rather than "what" you knew. Before taking the school exams I studied the three main Irish Sunday newspapers to find out when the major UK hospital recruiters would be in Cork. My brother dropped me off to Ashbourne House Hotel in Cork City. I asked if I could sit the exam there and then, since I wouldn't be collected for some hours. I was so happy to pass! Sometime later I flew to Luton Airport for an interview at St Albans City Hospital near London. Flying out of Ireland was a totally new and very big experience for me. My aunt and uncle brought me from the airport and we stayed overnight in London before the interview the next morning. I was surprised to be interviewed by a male nurse-tutor, but it went very well. I got the news that I had been accepted for training before I received my Leaving Certificate results.

Nursing training started at the end of August. It was a three-year traditional training carried out through a combination of working on the wards and regular block sessions of formal education. Looking back, it seems to me that this form of training was so much more beneficial for patient well-being. It was patient care oriented, rather than the more clinical and clerical roles played by nurses today.

It was all a total culture shock for me in 1988. At first it was the strangeness of being amongst a group of English girls of mostly 17 or 18 years old. Some of them were engaged and most of them were having sex. This was certainly not the way Irish girls of that age behaved in Ireland. The food was totally different too. Although we lived in nurses' homes and we had to look after our own meals, we were paid monthly and not used to budgeting, so we were often rather hungry in the weeks before payday. Sometimes we even gave blood because we knew we would be given biscuits after. I was a shy girl and very conscious of my Irish accent. These two things combined to make me seem a little remote and perhaps abrupt to others. When this was remarked upon, it did not help my confidence. However, within a year I was used to my new lifestyle and enjoying it. We worked hard on eight-hour shifts five days a week, with every second weekend worked. Although I had a best friend in London and two of my brothers over there, I still flew back to Ireland three or four times a year to see my friends. I also became friends with two other Irish girls on the same floor of the nurses' home and we would go out together in London on Sunday nights to the National[10]. As it happened two of my nursing classmates ended up marrying men that they met through school friends of mine working in construction in London.

In England during the IRA[11] attacks in the 1990's it was very awkward because sometimes I felt that my Irish accent might be seen to link me to them. On one occasion I was in a local bank just a few hours before the IRA bombed it. On another, someone said to me, "I see your crowd have been at it again last night". Innocent Irish friends had been pulled in for questioning. It was very unnerving and it was one aspect of why I didn't really enjoy living in England at the time. Eventually I came back to

---

[10] National Ballroom, Kilburn
[11] Irish Republican Army

Ireland to live in 1997 after nine years away. I decided to go travelling soon after and went with a friend to Australia for a year. We returned in 1998 to find Ireland completely changed in the ten years we had been away. When we were young we never went out to eat in restaurants or had foreign holidays. In previous times an outing usually consisted of a drive on Sunday to visit relatives. Our diet had been mainly spuds, bacon, cabbage, carrots, chicken and chops. Now most people seemed to be taking a sun holiday and dining out regularly. The variety of foodstuffs and other goods available in the shops had increased a great deal and mobile phones were becoming common. Signs of an economic boom were becoming evident and many of my peers were returning to Ireland.

During my year in Australia, I met my Irish husband, and when we returned we settled in my old village with my children attending the same school that I did. I am still enjoying my nursing career, unlike the nurses prior to 1973, who had to give up their jobs once married. And I often say to my children, "Let's sit down and have a chat in the garden for twenty minutes".

****

Jennifer Sleeman

Although I did not come to Ireland until the 1950's when my husband retired from the British Army, I have become the matriarch of a very Irish family. Five of my six children and their families live here and all six identify themselves as Irish.

At the time of my arrival here I was the young mother of three of my six children, after a childhood in South Africa and an early adulthood as an Army wife on the continent. We came to Ireland because it was the home of a very close friend of my husband's (they had been prisoners of war together) and he recommended it as a good place to live. Certainly, I would endorse this and have never for a moment been anything but grateful for the life we have here. My children are all staunchly Irish and love being so, as the Irish are always greeted as friends anywhere in the world.

Of course, initially, there were differences for me to get used to. When I had my fourth child in a nursing home in the late 1950's I was astonished that no one was breast-feeding and that all the patients gathered to say the rosary together every night. In those days, new mothers were not allowed to take baths and it was assumed that sleeping pills would be taken at night. My fifth child's normal birth was another surprise when I was anaesthetised for the birth without being consulted. However, we did feel very welcomed in Ireland and people were kind to us. I joined the ICA to get to know others and found the monthly meetings very friendly and informative.

When I was small we would say our simple prayers at night, but only when we visited my mother's people in Scotland did we go to church. I clearly remember the minister giving a very loud sermon, shouting, and thinking it must be me he was shouting at. I was terrified although I don't think I told anyone. God was someone we did not worry about until World War 2 came and my mother, with three children, sailed from South Africa to the UK to join our father who was recalled to the Navy. We thought it would be a great adventure to be torpedoed and prayed each night that God would make this happen! How wise our mother was not to tell us what the reality of being torpedoed would be like and how good that our prayers were not answered.

During the war, we went to the Church of England and when we moved north, to the Church of Scotland. I remember the first Sunday when there were no bells, as bells were to tell us the invasion had begun.

Back in South Africa post-war I now considered myself grown-up and I seemed to have been quite religious driving 14 miles to the little thatched Anglican Church on Sundays. The only thing I remember about that was an old lady sitting in front of me and the feather in her hat bobbing to the beat of her heart, and some pleasure in the prayers. Then I married a Catholic and had to promise that the children would be brought up in the faith. I did notice the comfort and pleasure that my husband got from his religion and considered changing, but it was only when I came to live in North Cork that I found a priest who was interested enough to give me instruction. After a year of instruction and discussion with Father O'Neill every Tuesday evening I was received into the church. He was a wonderful old man; I loved him dearly and cried bitter tears at his funeral. I must state quite clearly that, as I am now and the church was then, I would not have joined, but I must have been different then.

In 1972, we moved to a house with a field in Ardfield. By then my sons were away at college, my older daughters boarding at school in Dunmanway and my youngest in the

National School at Rathbarry. Over the years I kept hens, ducks, turkeys, goats, ponies and geese and found the hayshed useful for drying washing. It was important to me all my life to be self-sufficient, the way our family had been on the farm in South Africa. Even as a child I had kept my own rabbits and hens. So many people there would say, 'We got everything off the place' and it was something I aspired to which was not possible in the mobile Army life. I read John Seymour's book Self Sufficiency while at Ardfield and it made a big impression on me, and added to my intense interest in sustainability and taking care of the environment.

Thinking back to the days of being a mother my life seemed to be full of growing food and preparing it for consumption by my family. In Ardfield we took part in the 'Stations', the custom of hosting Mass in rotation around the farmhouses of the townland. How often the stations were held in your own home depended on how many Catholic families were in the farmhouses of the townland, but it was not expected of the cottages. It was about every ten years in our area at the time. At the last stations I held, the priest arrived when I had the pre-dinner nibbles arranged on the table and before the main course was out of the oven. "Is this all we are going to eat?" he asked with concern. Stations were a great way of socialising with all your neighbours and everyone was invited to call in over the course of the day. The festivities would go on long after the Mass was said and the meal eaten. Far into the night visitors would be welcomed with food and drink.

I think to begin with I had Faith and the Church gave me sustenance, but slowly things began to change. I applied to CMAC (now known as ACCORD). This is where, very late in life, I gained confidence to be myself and know that I had certain abilities, and for this opportunity I will always be grateful to the church. Sadly, as time went on into the 1980's, my husband's mind began to fail noticeably. Increasing forgetfulness and perhaps some depression resulted in being referred to a geriatrician. The diagnosis was delivered like a bombshell: it was Alzheimer's. And with nothing else said, we were shown the door. What to do? I was shell-shocked but wrote to my sisters in the UK and they sent me information. Later, I corresponded with the specialist we saw and explained how difficult it was to deal with such news without any information or support on the future and coping, offered. He agreed and apologised and thankfully things changed for the better. In those times, it was hard to break the news to people about mental conditions. I remember one very nice man asking, 'How is the Colonel?' When I explained that something had gone very wrong with his mind he kindly said, 'What a sad thing to happen to such a nice gentleman.'

Meanwhile faith continued to fade and although I still go to Mass I wonder if I should. It all seems irrelevant in the overpopulated world (and here the church must bear some guilt) poised on environmental collapse. I find the Church is full of rules made up by old celibate men and has little to say to the present world and its problems.

There have been glimpses of what could be, Mass in Peru where I wept at the power of devotion tangible in the church. Mass in Knocknaheeny where my great friend Pat Fogarty is PP and where the Church feels welcoming and alive. Mass in Glenstal: the richness of the liturgy.

After my husband died I moved into Clonakilty town because I was on my own. It was one of the best things I ever did because for the first time in my adult life I came to feel that I belonged and was part of a real and vibrant community. I became involved in working to raise awareness in issues important to me and that has been a great source of satisfaction and new friendships.

****

A typical well to do country dresser.

Carole Murphy

I first came to Clonakilty from England in 1964. It was the hometown of an Irish friend I made while working as a registered nurse in the Chelsea Pensioner's Hospital in London. We came over together several times on holiday, travelling by boat and car and stayed with her family.

I was surprised to see what a big influence the domestic troubles that Ireland suffered had on the development of the country. Shops and homes were so much more modest than I was used to while growing up in England. Although most homes had electricity, many still brought in water in buckets from the rainwater barrel or pump in the street. Linoleum was more common a floor covering than carpet and furniture was simple. The roads and streets were less developed with few streetlights about.

In 1966, I returned again to work as a nurse in the Bandon Cottage Hospital and later in the Bandon Nursing Home. I really liked Ireland and enjoyed coming back. Although I never thought I had any Irish blood, I was once told that my great grandmother's parents, by the name of Hayes, went over to England from Cork during the times of the Irish Famine.

A group of us frequently went to the ballroom dances held at the Industrial Hall at the Clonakilty Showgrounds, or in marquees erected on the field at Faxbridge during the summer festivals. Crowds would turn up for them either on foot or bicycle, because cars were not commonly owned then. Being used to the hours the English kept, I initially had trouble getting used to the late starting times of the dances. Once I went at 9pm and the band had not yet arrived. People thronged in after the shops and pubs had closed. There was no alcohol sold at the dances. Men lined one side of the venue and women the other and the dancing all happened in the middle. The bands played popular Irish ballads and country style music. Nothing else was provided other than the venue, music and minerals to drink, and the dancing went on until one or two in the morning.

At one of the frequent Dunmore House ballad sessions I met a Clonakilty shopkeeper. After a period of going out together to ceilis, pubs and summer festivals we got engaged and then married in England in 1968. Looking back a rather humorous thing happened to us at the time. Before returning to Ireland where buying and/or importing contraceptives was illegal, we decided to purchase a supply of condoms to take back with us. Outside the shop, being a little shy at never having done this before, we had a bit of a discussion as to who should go in to buy them. Eventually we decided to do it together. We bought hundreds of them and hid them in a gramophone cabinet we were bringing back with us. It was quite a nerve-wracking thing to do at the time and I was so very worried that we would be caught. As soon as we got back we hid them in the attic. The irony was that we didn't discover them again until years later, when we were renovating the attic to make a playroom for the children. So much time had elapsed by then that all we could think of to do was to dump them.

Although my father-in-law owned a shoe shop on Pearse Street, he had set my husband up in an electrical business on the opposite side of the street. There he sold washing machines, cookers, radios, toys, jewellery, refrigerators, souvenirs, and television sets, the latter being also rented out. Because we had the electrical shop we were one of the first families in town to have a TV[12] in 1968.

_____

12 The President of Ireland, Eamon de Valera launched the new television service on Sunday December 31,1961 and warned that, "...never before was

After we were married we lived on the top floor above my father-in-law's shoe shop as someone else occupied the first-floor flat. This was the home that our first-born twin girls and subsequent daughter came to. After three or four years there we were lucky enough to win a Mini[13] car in a festival raffle. We sold it in order to renovate an outhouse behind the shoe shop and make a new kitchen, dining and living area and we went upstairs to the bedrooms. Also, out the back of the shop, across a cobbled lane, there was a very old disused bake house with rows of ovens, in which we used to keep our gun dogs. Shooting pheasants and widgeon was a hobby that later led to breeding dogs for gundog trials. After 12 years living at the shop we moved along with our two little sons to a new house in Clogheen, where we lived for another 12 years before moving to Kent Street. Our lovely home there, which we later regretted selling, became the Town Hall.

The electrical shop was sold after my father in law died in 1986 and we then took over running the shoe shop. Our shoe shop was typical of the time with a long counter as you went in the door. There was only a very small selection of shoes on display in the window in those days. All the shoes were kept in boxes and people explained the type of shoes and size they needed. We sold slippers, wellingtons, waders, steel capped work boots, sandals, school and dress shoes. The assistant, who bought out the shoes for the customer to try, sat on a special a little stool with a slope on it for the customer's foot. The customer was helped into the shoes using a curved shoe-horn inserted at the heel. Sales were rung up on an old time manual cash

there in the hands of men an instrument so powerful to influence the thoughts and actions of the multitude."

[13] The British Motor Corporation produced Mini, was the iconic small car of the 1960's. It was the first front wheel drive car and its fuel efficiency made it affordable to drive.

register. This register is sometimes still seen today decorating the shop window on special occasions. I worked for an hour or two as needed in the shoe shop. My nursing was given up when the children arrived, as most of my time was spent caring for them.

A lot of shops had the long counters at the front then, with the assistants standing behind them. There were also lots of small grocery shops in the town. One grocery shop had a fireplace in the middle of the shop and seats around the walls on which you could wait while your order was filled. Sugar, flour, and biscuits came in big tins and were weighed out to order and bagged. Another grocery shop sold alcohol as well, so you could refresh yourself with "a drop" while you waited. There was also a lady on Ashe Street who cooked hot chips, which she sold from what would have been the living room of her house. She also had a juke-box, so it was a popular place for young people to go to. On Saturdays, the shops opened from 9am until 10pm at night. There used to be a real buzz in the town on Saturdays as people made a day-out of it. I used to do most of my own shopping in Clonakilty in order to support our fellow business owners, but when we also acquired the shop in Bandon, I supported them too. Most of the shops were closed on Wednesdays and also every Show Day.

After I had been living in Clonakilty a while, I joined the local Ladies Club which met at O'Donovan's Hotel. It was a nice way to spend time with other women. We had a series of speakers and there was also a drama group I was interested in. One time a speaker came from the Red Cross to talk about First Aid and Home Nursing and said that Clonakilty should have its own group. As I had an interest in the work of Red Cross, having been a member in England since the age of 16, I somehow ended up becoming the President of the new local chapter. However, before I had even arranged the first meeting I had a crisis to manage. The Postman sought me out and told me that about 60 refugees from the North of Ireland were soon to be arriving in the town. This was at the time of the Troubles in Northern Ireland. I later learned that the refugees probably resulted from the controversial British Army operation in Belfast on August 9th and 10th, 1971, known as "Operation Demetrius". These women and children had seen their men roughly seized from their homes and put into internment without trial because they were suspected of being involved with Irish Republican paramilitaries. The families had to leave with only the clothes they stood up in and were sent to refugee camps in the Republic. These people were to be set up and cared for in accommodation at the Convent and Darrara College. As President of the local Red Cross I was rather shocked to learn that I had to co-ordinate the arrangements. I was a very nervous public speaker but had to call a big town meeting in O'Donovan's Hotel to get things organised. Many of the mothers and children had no shoes and such inappropriate clothing for the very hot weather that some suffered from heat stroke. The supplies, along with basic items like soap and sanitary towels, had to be obtained from Cork.

There were many more children than women. In one place, I remember there were about 40 children to eight women. Help was needed to ensure that all the little ones were fed and I helped out with this and as I had my own small children to look after, they came along too. The families stayed in Clonakilty for several months before dispersing and a few remained for good.

I continued to teach First Aid, home nursing and bandaging and attend local sports matches etc. for quite some time afterwards.

A Kent St Town Hall window with old town hall and photographer reflected. Clonakilty no longer has a Town Council but does have publicly elected mayors for ceremonial purposes.

Business Woman

Sad circumstances resulted in me becoming a businesswoman, when my husband died suddenly in the 1980's. Our livelihood came from my husband's successful company and it seemed the right thing to do to carry it on. Fortunately, I had some experience of the commercial world from studying accounting and working in a Cork company, but that was some years earlier. I had also been working with my husband on some of the technical aspects of the enterprise ever since we were married. Already I had some of the key attributes like; good English, people skills and was developing an eye for graphics. However, during that time I worked office hours and went home with no worries, but with his passing the latter was no longer possible.

The business involved heavy lifting of materials and work with machinery, so it was very much a man's world. I was not sure that I would be able to cope but decided to give it my all. Life was not easy but I poured every bit of energy I had into the business. I was a local Clonakilty girl from a large family and while none of them had experience in the work I was now doing, they were wonderful in that they helped me, by working with me, otherwise the business survival would not have been possible.

Back then there were no organisations for business-women in Clonakilty that encouraged networking or sharing of issues and ideas. Before my husband passed away, I was a member of the Clonakilty Ladies Club for a few years. It was a social group that allowed me to meet a cross section of people outside my normal family and work circles. From them I picked up new skills in effective communication and the ability to feel confident in speaking up for things that were important to me. I also gained an understanding of how organisations are run efficiently. It was business-like but also fun.

I had to quickly develop a number of new skills. It was very important to become shrewd enough, in such a masculine domain, to be able to discern the type of people I was dealing with in order to avoid being conned. It was necessary to become adept at meeting client deadlines, ensuring there was enough money in the bank to meet all contingencies, and above all to ensure that the customer was always totally satisfied. Knowledge of the difficult art of costing had to be gained via a FAS course. Dealing with competition was another skill to be developed. All through this period we had no more than three or four staff, but I was extremely lucky to have an offer of help from a knowledgeable friend of my late husband. This was invaluable at the time and consequently he became a very good and trusted employee.

I was honoured to be co-opted on to the Clonakilty Town Council. When the next election was held I was elected by popular vote, which was a big surprise to me. The Town Council work helped me a lot in that it gave me a focus outside my business and the opportunity to think about others and move forward in my life. In time, I became the Council representative on The Clonakilty Enterprise Board and its Chairperson for some years.

One of the hardest things for me to do was asking for money from the banks to finance new machinery. I had to be assertive and strong. People were all very good to me and I cannot speak highly enough of the people of Clonakilty. Another big challenge in our business was adapting to the new technological era. There was a great deal to be learned and it is on-going with the continuing advances in technology. One change that makes life easier relates to the ordering and collection of materials. Once done by phone or a salesman calling, with personal collection required by ourselves, now an email is sent and they are delivered to the door.

In those earlier days men commonly viewed women in business on their own with a suspicion that they could not possibly be equal to the job. This belief was reinforced by the 1937 Irish Constitution, which infers that a woman's place is in the home. It was not unknown for some male suppliers and customers to say, "It is very nice to meet you, but I would like speak to the boss?" This attitude has now changed somewhat with so many women working outside the home, although there is still a shortage of women in government. I have come to appreciate that, in general, both men and women bring different but complementary strengths to the job, men are naturally more confident and assertive with bold decisions, while women are very thorough and attentive to the fine detail.

However, the new generation of young women are very well educated and qualified. When asked if I have any advice for women in business, I say that I think that they must be committed to lifelong learning, patient about rising to the top and ready to make the difficult decisions that may not make them popular, especially where financial matters are concerned. Life can be very rough when people let you down and money is left outstanding. I would suggest that women thinking of creating their own business go away and get the necessary qualifications, then work experience with someone else, and then go into business on their own. I also think that patience, kindness and appreciating your clients and the work that they give you, is a big help.

It was not easy for me being a mother, housewife and businesswoman all rolled into one. At times, I felt very lonely and sometimes a bit cross that I had been left in this position. But in many ways the business was my salvation. I just had to get on with it. Being busy along with the enjoyment of feeling satisfied with the contribution I was making helped a lot with my grieving process. I love my job and now in 2015 I am still going into the office most days. I feel that I have been very lucky overall. The recession years of the new millennium were a cruel blow and devastating floods in recent years have been huge setbacks to our business, which was inundated, but the supportive and compassionate Clonakilty community always do what they can for you. It is greatly appreciated.

Noreen Minihan

My father was one of the first Garda Siochana in Clonakilty when he came to the barracks on Pearse St in 1922. It was on the site occupied today by Galwey's Pharmacy. My mother lived at 58 Pearse St and so they met and married and I was their firstborn child. Sadly, my father died just four months later from pneumonia, brought on by getting thoroughly soaked while helping out at a time of flooding.

My mother ran a highly successful grocery business. Her entrepreneurial spirit expressed itself when she opened a restaurant in our dining room, behind the shop. It was a very busy venture, especially on Friday Market days and Fair days (which were held on the first Monday of the month) and required staff to help her. She was especially known for her cream cakes and tarts, bought from local bakeries. My grandmother, who lived with us, was a noted dressmaker and instructed girls in the art of dressmaking. When I was about six years old Mammy remarried a wonderful man, and had five more children. After her death, her shop was named Betty Brosnan's after her.

All my schooling took place in Clonakilty. The nuns were very good to me at secondary school. Knowing that it was all hands-on deck to help out in the shop after school, they encouraged me to bring two lunches to school each day. This way, plus a sustaining cup of tea, I could stay on at school to study until 6pm. After completing my Leaving Certificate (a requisite for a career in teaching, nursing or the Civil Service: the main avenues open to women) I began my training at Mary Immaculate Teachers' Training College in Limerick. My teachers from Sacred Heart were delighted, as it was an honour for the school to have a pupil accepted there.

I started in 1949 and in those days the student teachers, all girls, lived in. There were 100 students: 50 juniors and 50 seniors. It was a very regimented and rather Spartan life, up at 6.30am and to bed at 9.00pm. Another avenue into teaching for those not accepted into training college, was through becoming a Junior Assistant Mistress (JAM). In the Leaving Certificate year girls could take optional Easter oral exams. If you passed the exams, which covered English, Irish, needlework and singing, you could obtain teaching work in a school if the average number of pupils was low (say 8-10 students). The pay was less than that of a trained teacher, but in fact, if student numbers were low, even a trained teacher only received the JAM salary.

My career as a teacher began at Knockskeagh School, about 7 kilometres from Clonakilty. My mother bought me a beautiful state of the art bicycle. It had three speed gears, a dynamo lamp, a basket in the front, a carrier at the back and a bicycle stand! It was the envy of all the pupils. To this day past pupils talk about my 'Merc'[14] of a bike!

In 1955, I transferred to St Joseph's Infant Boys' School in Clonakilty. The Infant School consisted of three classes: Junior Infants (four and five-year olds) Senior Infants (six) and First Standard (seven year olds). It was located in lovely old cut stone buildings in O'Rahilly Street, opposite Scoil na mBuachaillí today. In 1955 my class consisted of 56 junior and senior infant boys, with desks and seating for just 38! I managed to accommodate them by rotation, having some seated on the floor for listening tasks, some at the desks for written work and the rest standing for blackboard work. Because all the pupils started on their fourth birthday, in a later year just before the summer break, I had 62 children in the class. However, sometime later the system changed to one where all the children

---

[14] Short for Mercedes, a luxury car of the day.

started at the beginning of the school year after they had turned four.

In 1957 the Public Service Marriage Bar was lifted for teachers and so when I married in 1959 I was able to continue. My husband, Michael, was a travelling representative for Deasy's Brewery, which at that time was bottling Guinness and manufacturing Deasy Minerals in premises under the arch and at the back of O'Donovan's Hotel on Pearse St. It later moved to what is now known as Deasy's Car Park and then to Cork. We had six children, three boys and three girls between 1960 and 1972 and I worked up until the day each baby was born. We got precisely six weeks maternity leave before we had to return to work. They were very busy years, but we had a housekeeper to help. I did all the knitting of jumpers and cardigans for the family in any moment where I was sitting down and also a great deal of sewing for the girls and the occasional special outfit for the boys. The play-pen was a very handy thing to have: I got into it myself with a small table, seat and my sewing machine.

In 1963 the Infant School moved to the new school buildings across the road and I became the Principal of the Infant School in 1967, a position I held until 1995. When the job of Principal of the amalgamated Infant and Senior School came up in 1995 I was offered the role, but instead chose to continue teaching for my final year as a permanent employee, before retirement in 1996. I continued on as a substitute teacher in various schools in West Cork, often at very short notice, until Michael took ill in 2008. Thus, I can say that I have taught many a local man under the age of 62 at some stage. It was a job I loved, particularly preparing the 7 year olds for their first Holy Communion. I now have the title of Diocesan Visitor, which involves talking to the pupils about what they have learned in the Religion Programme.

Alongside my career I was also involved as secretary for the Irish National Teachers Organisation from the day I left training college and was not relieved until I had four children.

My husband and I believed it important to take part in the local community and action groups enabling progress and improvements that benefit everyone both practically and socially. We were very involved in the Festivals of West Cork in the 1960's and 1970's and I was the Hostess in the highly popular Midnight Cabarets. Some of the more important activities I was part of were:

- From 1964 fundraising for the Cork Polio Aftercare group, which over time became COPE.
- The Children of Mary, Catholic Religious Association.
- Community fundraising for the building of the Clonakilty Community Hall, which opened in 1983 at a cost of £379,000.
- Clonakilty Tidy Towns, a chapter of a national organisation to stimulate pride of place for residents, workers and visitors from the end of the 1970's. I am currently President of Clonakilty Tidy Towns.
- CLOAG, the Clonakilty Local Organisation Action Group which helped Travellers out of crowded barrel topped roadside caravans and tents and into local authority houses. A preschool was also set up to assist the children to make friends before they got to school. Later state funding helped with training and the establishment of the Traveller's Centre.
- Training boys and girls to serve at Mass and religious ceremonies.

- Organising a lottery to enable on-going funding for the Clonakilty Community Hospital and the local Community Hall.

Each of these organisations, thanks to all the willing workers involved, has made a positive contribution to the town and its people over the years as well as being a source

of friendship and pleasure for me.

Clonakilty Catholic Church

Four Generations of Clonakilty Women

With Thea Ryan, assisted by her extended family.

My family and I live in a unique Clonakilty semi-detached house, which was built in 1904. I am the fourth generation in the maternal line of my family who has lived in this house during the last 113 years. For much of my life, I have lived in one side or the other, along with other members of my family.

Susan Helen Fitzpatrick (1877-1950)

Two bachelor brothers were tenants on land adjacent to Desert House and wished to purchase the rented land from my great-grandparents. The Fitzpatricks had no wish to part with the property, so the brothers frequently harassed and bullied them when they returned from town (possibly drunk) late at night. Susan believed that the stress of living alongside these unpleasant neighbours was the reason that she was unable to sustain her pregnancies and expand their family. Despite at least five miscarriages Susan and John Fitzpatrick raised only two

children, Martha, known as Lilian or Lily, and Samuel, both of whom were born in Desert House.

Susan's brother Richard (Dick) Helen travelled to America with her husband, John James Fitzpatrick sometime around the turn of the 20th Century. John James had an interest in architecture, as his father had been involved in the plans for the Clonakilty Courthouse and both the local Methodist and Presbyterian churches. On their return Susan instigated the building of two adjoining houses in Clonakilty using plans sourced by her brother and husband on the American trip. They named the building Western Villas. Susan, John James and Dick had a great deal of input into the building of the semi-detached houses. One of the villas became the Fitzpatrick home and Susan's bachelor brother Dick lived in the other. They took up residence on their completion in 1904. The Fitzpatrick's little girl, Martha, who became known as Lily or Lilian Fitzpatrick, was my grandmother. Eventually part of the land at Desert was sold to displace the bothersome tenant brothers, but many years later it was brought back into family ownership.

Lilian (Martha) Fitzpatrick Winter (1904 – 1990)

My grandmother Lily received her education in Cork at the Rochelle School, a school established in 1829 to make educated young ladies of the daughters of the merchants, professionals and businessmen in the Church of Ireland community. Most of the staff comprised lay teachers who educated boarding and day pupils. It became known as the Rochelle School when it moved to the gardens of Rochelle House in 1863 on the road to Blackrock, Cork.

Lily returned to Clonakilty, on the completion of her education. O'Donovan's Hotel was then, as it is today, a social hub in the community. The card evenings, dancing and cocktail bar, drew many people together. Philip Winter, from Rathdown Road, Arran Quay in Dublin, travelled to Clonakilty in the course of his occupation as a Royal Insurance agent and he was introduced to Lily there. They both loved to dance and enjoyed each other's company greatly. It was inevitable that they would marry. Their wedding was held at St Finbarr's Cathedral, Cork City, in 1930.

We know little of Lily's early, married life, other than she was a lady who was always well dressed in beautiful clothes and very involved with her church. She played the organ and grew and arranged the weekly church flowers. She also loved to play the piano, knit (including jumpers for her grandchildren), sew, embroider, garden, bake and made her own jams and marmalade. I remember as a youngster if we were sent to Gran's she always had beautiful homemade soup (especially tomato soup) and brown soda bread. They had several apple trees with varieties for both eating and cooking and two greenhouses in the backyard at Western Villas where Lily and Philip grew their own vegetables, tomatoes and a grape vine. One of the greenhouses still exists today.

Dorothy Winter Jennings (1933-2014)

Lily and Philip's daughter, my mother Dorothy, was born in the Bon Secours Hospital in Cork city in 1933. When she was a little girl the family lived in Western Villas with her parents and grandparents. She was an only child, rather a tomboy and ahead of her time. When young she spent happy times playing outside on the road with some of the local boys and loved to cycle and ride horses. This eased the loneliness of spending so much time with just the kitchen maid for company. Dorothy used to tell us that she attended both the Methodist Church and the Church of Ireland every Sunday in Clonakilty, with her grandfather Fitzpatrick. Being an only child weighed heavily on my mother and she often spoke of her lonely early life. Apparently she told everyone that she was going to live in her Grandma's house at Desert one day and have a big family. That is exactly what she eventually did.

Around 1939 Dorothy's father, Philip Winter, was appointed to an administrative job in Bangor, Northern Ireland, due to his experience in the British Army in World War One. Philip was a Dispatcher and rode a motorbike with panniers carrying vital communications. He was Honourably Discharged from the British Army as he sustained wounds from shrapnel when near an explosion and as a consequence developed "The Shakes", known today as "Post Traumatic Stress Disorder". During WW2 it was safer for the family to be in Northern Ireland as

Philip was both in the British Army and a British Subject. It was said that Churchill was unsure of what Hitler might do in the Republic of Ireland, as it was an easy target. The Republic of Ireland was neutral at this time.

Dorothy spent four years in Bangor with her parents from ages six through to ten. She saw the boats gathered in the harbour just before D Day and knew something big was about to happen. Northern Ireland was used as one of the main bases for preparing for the D-Day Normandy landings in June 1944. She was also aware of the famous shipping manufacturers Harland and Wolfe and in later years their great gantry cranes known as Samson and Goliath, built in the late 1960's and early 70's which are still a feature of the Belfast cityscape. (The "Titanic Belfast" exhibition today, is housed in the old Harland & Wolfe shipyards where the ship was built.) Food was rationed during the war especially tea, sugar, flour and eggs. Dorothy's mother, Lily Winter, was renowned for her delicious drop scones made with dried egg powder during that time.

When the war ended in 1945 the family returned to Blackrock, Cork, as it was easier for her father to continue his Royal Insurance career from there and Dorothy attended Rochelle School. However shortly after their return from the North John James Fitzpatrick died. As Lily's mother Susan was now alone in Western Villas, Lily and Philip returned to live there, while Dorothy remained in Cork as a weekly boarder at Rochelle.

Dorothy was intelligent and a hard worker but she had very mixed feelings about her time at boarding school. She loved the company of the other pupils and learning. Reading widely was a passion, but there were unhappy memories and perhaps some homesickness and lack of freedom too, illustrated by her telling her own children, "I would never send a daughter of mine to boarding school."

She finished her primary schooling there and completed secondary school along with both the Intermediate Certificate in 1949 and Leaving Certificate in 1951. Dorothy did well enough in her exams to consider going into medicine at college but initially she engaged in relief school teaching and taught Sunday school. However, she didn't find teaching appealing enough to make it her career. Instead she opted to go to Skerries College Cork and undertake book keeping and secretarial courses including stenography; also known as shorthand, a symbolic way of fast, accurate recording of the spoken word. On completion Dorothy returned to Clonakilty. During this time, she engaged fully in the social life typical for a girl her age within the Church of Ireland community. When she was a teenager she and her mother used to show their Golden Cocker Spaniels and Collie dogs in the local agricultural shows which were a big part of the annual summer social life of a farming area. Her grand-uncle Richard (Dick) Helen had been Treasurer of the Clonakilty Agricultural Society from 1932-1937[15].

Dorothy obtained a responsible job working in Cork for a textile company, Sunbeam Wolsey[16]. She worked there from 1950 to 1957 and said, "I was better paid than any girl on The Mall" due to the responsibility of her position of paying all the wages. Her father drove her up and down to Cork but she often stayed in the city with cousins as her father needed the family car for transport while he continued to work representing Royal Insurance both in their office on The Mall and in the wider County Cork area.

---

[15] Ref.:http://www.irishshows.org/shows/c/clonakilty/about/
[16] Sunbeam Wolsey, which closed in 1995, was the hosiery-making offshoot of Dwyer & Co and employed 2,000 women at its peak.

Attending a social event in the Parochial Hall in Clonakilty led Dorothy to meet a rather handsome and charming young man from Dunmanway, John Jennings. He was "a bit of a rogue" as he liked to dance with the girls and then while waltzing around the corner he would let them go and they would go spinning, sometimes even falling. However, both parties seemed to enjoy this fun. Initially, Dorothy's family did not view him as a good prospect for their daughter. He was a farmer and at the time, most definitely considered socially inferior by her parents. Also, my mother had another suitor, a well to do gentleman who was totally besotted with her and in later years he would say to her "You left me on the shelf and you never took me down to dust me off!" That poor man never married as he waited for her, but she had only eyes and time for my Dad.

At this stage Desert House was rented and tenanted. When Dorothy and John's engagement was announced it featured on the front page of the Irish Times. They gave the tenants in Desert House notice and John moved in and began renovations. Before marriage, while Dorothy was still working, she would come down to Desert House after work and bring John's dinner over from her mother's kitchen in Clonakilty. In addition, she helped hand milk the two cows as well as renovate the house. Superstitious local people believed the house John and Dorothy were renovating was haunted because a light would often be seen shining from one of the unused front bedroom windows. However, John discovered that a crow had found its way into the room and was perching on the old-fashioned lever that turned on the light. The house was a very good size being three bedrooms, a parlour, a dining room and kitchen, but needed a lot of work. My parents built on an extension adding two extra bedrooms, a kitchen, breakfast room and a large utility room.

Dorothy had a Cork address from staying with her cousins that permitted her to marry in St Finbarr's Cathedral, as her parents had done. The wedding was in April 1957 at the Cathedral where Dorothy had sung in the

choir. She was the first girl to wear a wedding dress by designer of the times, Ib Jorgensen. The wedding reception was held at the Imperial Hotel on South Mall in Cork. Photographs of the happy couple were again featured on the front of the Irish Times and they were also shown boarding their plane in Cork to honeymoon in France and Switzerland. Dorothy kept all these precious mementoes and wrote a diary every day until she died.

After arriving back from their honeymoon, the couple moved into Desert House. Dorothy cooked the first meal for her husband on a two-ring gas stove. Apparently, she managed the potatoes all right, but not the fish. Dad was actually a better cook than she when they were first married because he was the youngest in his family and had spent a lot more time with his mother. Dorothy didn't know how to boil an egg because the kitchen maid in her childhood home did not want to teach her anything. She felt Dorothy was a lady and didn't need to learn. However, over time Mum taught herself to cook and became very accomplished at it. Dad was great at knowing how to make ends meet. He grew a large vegetable garden that made them almost self-sufficient in produce. In the late 1950's when the herd grew to five cows Mum's father bought them an electric milking machine.

Sunbeam, the company my mother had worked for in Cork, had an office in Bandon in the 1950's. Mum continued to work there for a while after she married, as she only needed to travel about twelve miles. I recall her saying that she was "the wage clerk" and they had to "get three girls to do her job when she left". The children arrived in 1959, 1960, 1962, 1964 and 1966. Apparently, my father John Jennings wanted to have six children and my grandmother Lily Winter said, "If you and Dorothy have another child Philip and I will emigrate to Australia!" So that is why there are five children in our family.

In 1966 my tireless mother started the Desert House Farmhouse B&B with two bedrooms available. It was one of the first in the area. She loved the work because she was passionate about people and looking after them. My earliest memory of my mother is from when I was about three years old watching her cook dinner in the Bed and Breakfast kitchen at Desert House on Clonakilty Bay. My youngest brother was only a baby at the time.

Dorothy was the homemaker and John the worker: soul mates that were brilliant together. Old friends of hers told me that, "Dorothy wasn't long in Desert House and she had friends over to afternoon tea and everything looked so lovely". The house was in both their names, which was not the norm at the time. Another example of their working things out together was that when a baby was born, Dorothy picked the boy's names and dad picked the girl's. She was a marvellous parent; she gave up her job in 1957 because she wanted to be there for us and later to do whatever we desired in terms of after school activities. Mum drove us up and down to Cork herself for ballet, Girl's & Boy's Brigade, swimming etc. If she couldn't do it herself for some reason, her parents Granny and Pop Winter, who lived in Western Villas, were close by enough to help. Our Dad's parents, Mr and Mrs William Jennings, lived in Dunmanway and used to visit us regularly, but never stayed over because the coastal air and sea mist affected Grandpa Jenning's chest.

During the early 1970's my parents Dorothy and John, decided to extend the B&B, which gave them extra bedrooms plus bathroom and shower units. This gave them seven guest bedrooms altogether. They also enlarged the dining area for the guests and made the family area at the back of the house bigger for us all.

Dorothy also believed strongly in giving back to the community. She was involved in the Mother's Union which focussed on things like homemaking, parenting, and helping each other out in times of need, also the Irish Countrywomen's Association, and was an early member of Clonakilty Red Cross. Going with her mother, Lily, to the Drama Group was pure enjoyment for her. She participated in both acting and script-writing plays that were performed at the Parochial Hall, GAA pavilion and Industrial Hall. Dorothy's grandfather John James Fitzpatrick was Church Secretary to the Select Vestry in the Church of Ireland, as was her father Philip Winter and Dorothy took the job over from him when he became ill, around 1973. She was secretary for 41 years up until she died in 2014. At that point, I took over the position that had been held by the family for three generations prior.

One of my earliest memories of life at home that demonstrates my parent's sense of humour was when the farm help was meant to be keeping an eye on my brother and me, while he was painting the shed. He gave us some red paint to apply to the door. It all started well and then one of us put a daub of paint on the other. And so, it continued until we were both covered in it, our faces, hands, arms, plus boots and clothes were liberally coated in red! Dad laughed and Mum put us both in the bath and scrubbed us. We were red before but we were even redder after the bath. She was very cross, but laughing underneath it all. I remember going to school the following day and being teased, as was my brother. Red seemed to be a colour that attracted me, as my mother told me of some other times that I was too young to recall. Once she had three-year-old me beautifully dressed in a fur coat and I found her red lipstick. The coat was ruined as both it and I, were covered in lipstick. A year or two later I found red shoe polish and hid behind the sofa and again painted myself red.

Mum worked running her own business with up to ten bedrooms available and did full board: bed, breakfast, lunch and dinner in the early 1970's to 80's before there were any restaurants in the town. In 1973, Mum set-off on a promotional trip to Brittany, trying to encourage the French to come to Ireland. Alone she took the five of us youngsters by car and ferry. We stayed in gîtes, hotels and campsites wherever we went. She was very brave. I only remember some of it and to this day I still write to Madame Berrou who was so very kind to us at that time. Over the years Dorothy went through some difficult times. Diana was very ill as a baby and Granny and Pop Winter reared the oldest boy for his first couple of years. This allowed Dorothy and John to devote their time to the care of Diana in Crumlin Hospital, Dublin. She now lives a healthy life. Coping with worry must been have been a frequent necessity especially when four of Dorothy's children were involved in no-fault car accidents on separate occasions and times. On one of these she was told that that 22-year-old, Thea, "would never walk again." Thanks to excellent care, I too proved the outlook wrong.

My mother also opened a field for horse drawn caravans that were very popular with German and French tourists and that led to the Caravan and Camping business. For six years her interest in tourism prompted her to act as Bord Failte[17] Secretary between 1986 -1992. She gave up the B&B in 2009 when my father became ill. He passed away in 2010. She missed him terribly and used to say, "John and I were soul-mates, I was the brains and he was the brawn." A grandson summed up my Dad by saying, "He was the quiet man in the corner, but the centre of the room". Dorothy kept the caravan and camping business going as this helped pass the summers for her with familiar faces coming and going. She lived out her life at Desert House until she took ill and spent the last two weeks in Bon Secours Hospital where she passed away on 11 September 2014.

Our amazing mother never saw a problem, only a solution. Her interest in life, current affairs, knowledge and experience, was extensive. Family events and celebrations were always good times with loads of fun and food. She loved people. Sharing her knowledge with visitors, family and friends was a delight to her and she specially enjoyed promoting her much-loved hometown, Clonakilty.

We will never forget her.

---

[17] Irish Tourism Organisation

Thea Jennings Ryan (1964 -)

I was named Dorothea after my grandmother but my Dad, John Jennings, decided to call me Thea to avoid confusion with Mum who was Dorothy.

I had a very happy upbringing. My parents were wonderful and always encouraged us to do many things. The five of us, my three brothers and one sister, all worked very hard during our long summer holidays from school helping my parents run both a busy farm and Farm Guest House. During the peak season, we had 10 rooms to service as well as cook and serve breakfast; lunch and dinner, sometimes up to 40 guests would be staying. The kitchen was always busy and certainly the heart of the home. Mum taught us all to cook and I was her main baker. All day Saturday I baked buns, cakes, breads, bracks[18] and biscuits for the family and the tourists. Baking is a most enjoyable and fun skill to have. However, no matter how busy we were, Mum always made sure we got to the beach at Inchydoney, Duneen or The Warren regularly, either with Mum and Dad, or Granny and Pop Winter. One of the adults always stayed with us to ensure that we were never left alone.

When I was aged seven I landed in hospital to have my appendix removed and after that experience all I wanted to be was a nurse, so after gaining the grades I needed in my Leaving Certificate I applied to The Adelaide School of Nursing in Dublin and after interview was accepted to train as a nurse. My parents encouraged me all the way and were so proud to be invited to the prize giving ceremony where I was awarded the overall prize for practical nursing. I thanked my Mum especially; as she had trained me well

---

[18] A sweet cake-like bread made with flour, eggs, sugar, spice and sultanas soaked in tea. Served sliced and buttered.

before reaching the hospital environment. She was a very well-educated woman, and certainly had high standards.

On Sunday 15th April 1973 my mother, Dorothy wrote in her diary "My dearly loved father Philip B. Winter died today at 7.30am, Mum and John with him". After my grandfather died, Lily was rather lonely so I stayed with her quite frequently in Western Villas to keep her company.

Back when I was 10, all I wanted was a pony, as we had an old horse, Dolly, that my dad owned and used for ploughing the fields. When Dolly was too old to work anymore, I was allowed to ride her. After annoying my parents through begging and pleading, they sent me off to a riding school for a week to see if I liked the pony and all the activities that went along with riding. I did. The pony 'Golden Ranger' was bought for my birthday but after a few weeks, he decided he would throw me off into the nettles when I was galloping in a field one day. My father encouraged me to climb back on the pony again but I was nervous of the pony, and he knew it. So, Golden Ranger was given to my brother who made a good hand of him and won many prizes with him.

My sister remembers that when the Drama group Mum belonged to put on a play or drama, we would both be roped in to do a dance/ballet while the company would be changing sets or costumes. I recall wearing black leotards and black tights and thinking that we were absolutely fabulous while we pranced around the stage. Goodness knows what we did, but we did have some fun, based on the ballet training we had received at that time.

When we started going out with friends our Mum never put a time limit on our return. She had a bad experience when courting. Cycling back from Kilgarriffe to town, my father flew on ahead to get her home in time. She came off her bicycle, hurt herself and broke the bicycle. Her father was waiting at home and very angry with her for being late.

Not wanting her own children to experience the same, she only insisted that we woke her when we came in, to put her mind at rest. She was also lovely in that you could always talk to her about anything and if she didn't know the answer would refer you to her mother, who was also very knowledgeable. Sometimes when we wanted something special from Dorothy she would say, "Go and ask your father". Then Dad would say, "What did your mother say?" The only hard and fast rule was that we were not allowed motorbikes.

After my four years in Dublin (from 1982 to 1986) and Head Staff Nurse for a year, I returned to Cork to do my midwifery training in the Erinville Hospital. However, it was not to be. Three months into my training, I was driving home one dark wet evening on 13 November 1986 and was involved in a head on collision (not my fault). This resulted in being hospitalised for a long period, I sustained multiple injuries from fractured skull, to fractured limbs, burns, facial lacerations and broken teeth. My one vivid memory was when I regained consciousness my parents were looking over me and saying, "We are here, you will be fine". This was just before I was wheeled into the operating theatre and how right they were!

My recovery was very slow both mentally and especially physically. While in hospital my brother had an accident at work when steel fell on him and tore his ligaments so he landed in the same unit as I was in. It was fun because he would come and visit me each day, which helped shorten the days for the two of us. When I was eventually discharged from hospital, Mum or Dad had to drive me up and down the road to Cork for regular physiotherapy so that I would be able to walk again. Two years later I returned to nursing but found it too difficult for my legs, so I returned home to help with the family business. This is when I really spent a lot of time with my dear Mum, a dear friend as well as my Mum.

At the age of 16, I met the love of my life, David Ryan, at the West Cork Rally, while he was staying in the guesthouse with friends of our family. We married in 1990. When we got engaged my Mum offered me one of the two houses of Western Villas as a starter home until we decided where we were actually going to live. I fondly remember the day Mum and I went to buy my wedding dress in Cork. She had suggested I wear her own Ib Jorgensen dress, a

top designer of Danish origin between the years 1950-1990, but the dress unfortunately, didn't suit. We had such fun together trying on wedding gowns and "going away"[19] outfits.

David and I were married on 21st June 1990 at Kilgarriffe Church of Ireland and the reception was at the hotel at Courtmacsherry with 99 guests present. The 90-year-old grandmother of my husband-to-be asked, "Why did you pick the shortest night of the year to get married?" Also on that day Ireland beat The Netherlands in World Cup Football, so the guests were jubilant making for a great atmosphere. There was a big screen at the reception before the dancing started.

---

[19] A dressy outfit to wear when leaving for the honeymoon.

The happy days of our honeymoon came to an abrupt end when I received a telephone call with the sad news that my dear grandmother Lily had passed away on 5th July 1990. I just couldn't take in the news: she was at our wedding and enjoyed the whole day. On our return from our honeymoon it was straight into a funeral and so many of our wedding guests were present. I felt so numb that day! My grandmother Lily was like a second Mum to me, so kind and she taught me so very many things. She was seldom cross, but her pet hate was when someone would add an "s" to her last name. "It is 'Winter', there is no "s", she would say, "Will they ever get it right?"

I returned with David to live in Western Villas following our marriage. Over time we fell in love with the house and decided to buy the house from my Mum, as it was hers alone, having been left to her via her grandmother and mother in turn. We bought it at a gift price and have since spent quite a lot of money doing it up. I feel very fortunate to be living in a home that has been lived in by our family for generations. We decided to call our side Cranfield because the layout of our home reminded my husband's parents of Cranfield, the house of his grand-uncle, a bank manager in Limerick.

My parents were both super hosts and adored family gatherings and events, which they always celebrated and provided food and entertainment for all. After each grandchild was born, 16 in total, they always visited the hospital together to greet the new arrival. They loved to come to our place for the children's birthdays and over the Christmas period and we would have fun playing games, cards (Bridge, Forty-five and Whist) and just being together. Never did my Mum forget a birthday or anniversary, she was so generous to everyone. I am so happy that my children, her grandchildren, had quality time with her. She loved people and places and always showed interest in other people's lives and families and was a great advisor. Many people to this day say how much they miss Dorothy and I must say she still is a huge void in my daily life.

I still live in my ancestors' home, it has served three generations and we are now the fourth. My children love its character and features. They were born in 1993, 1996, 1999, and 2001 in the Erinville Hospital, Cork.

I feel grateful and privileged to be one link in this chain of spirited women who make up my family tree and were very much part of the fabric of Clonakilty life.

Mary Ruth McCarthy

Sam Glanville, my father, was a lighthouse keeper, as was his father before him and we lived a somewhat roaming life as we moved about the Irish Coast. He and my mother Jo were from the south of Ireland; Michael my brother (born 1930), Martha my sister (born 1933) and I (born 1932) were all born near Kilkeel, Co. Down. A lighthouse keeper had to have experience of life at sea, or a trade, in order to undertake the training for light keeping and my father had both.

In 1936 we lived in Inishowen, Co. Donegal, then moved to Cobh, Co. Cork in 1939 where my father 'kept the light' on Spitbank in the harbour. Furnished dwellings were provided on site, for keepers' families, the exception being Cobh. Here we lived in rented accommodation. This consisted of a large house divided in two. I called it 'half a house', because another family occupied the other half. There was a large garden behind the house, very sheltered, so apple trees and fruit bushes thrived, and there was plenty of ground space to grow potatoes, onions carrots etc. In 1942 we moved to Skerries, Co. Dublin. The lighthouse was on Rockabill, some way off the Dublin coast.

In December of the same year we made our next and final move to Galley Head Lighthouse situated on a headland, eight or nine miles from Clonakilty town, West Cork. Back then this location was seen as somewhat isolated and consequently backward. My mother was very concerned about Michael's secondary schooling. It was accepted in those days that a girl's further education was of less importance.

Near the houses at Galley Head there was a huge rainwater tank and a cold-water tank in the pantry that had a sink. My mother cooked on the coal range in the kitchen. We also had a Scandinavian primus stove for quick cooking. She made delicious beef stews, Irish stews, and frequently cooked fish; mackerel or the less favoured pollock. My father caught the fish from a rowing boat with a friend, or from the rocks with rod but no reel. Although we ate rashers as a treat for Sunday breakfast, we seldom ate pork in any form, as there were disease concerns about its consumption at the time.

The only form of transport we had was my father's bicycle, my mother never cycled. She was taken to town once or twice a month in the local farmer's horse and cart, or occasionally in a pony and trap. My father wore a uniform provided, but clothes for the rest of the family came from Cash's and O'Mahoneys, drapers on Rossa Street. We did not have modern conveniences so we washed ourselves in a galvanised bath in front of the fire.

The Galley Head had a telephone line, possibly because of its coastal monitoring role in wartime. Occasionally a local person came to use the telephone to ask for the doctor or vet to be called out. The Second World War was raging in Europe at the time, although Ireland was not involved its Government co-operated with the Allies. There was rationing of clothes, tea, cigarettes etc.

The nomadic life we lived we enjoyed very much. This meant we attended four very different primary schools. All Michael ever wanted to do was 'go to sea' and following two years attendance (by bicycle) at St. Mary's Secondary School in Clonakilty, this is what he did. Martha died before her 15th birthday; this was a very sad time for us.

Following my father's retirement, we continued to live in West Cork. I spent some years in England, first as a teacher in Kidderminster and then nurse training in Birmingham, later returning to Ireland where I worked as a nurse.

My husband Jerry and I married in 1961, raising our six daughters and two sons in rural West Cork. Our great treat in those days was to take a picnic and go by car to the seaside often visiting Galley Head Lighthouse, seen below. *The following is a true story written by Mary Ruth, about her memories of a real event.*

My father opened the door of the bedroom where Martha

and I slept and, as if it were an everyday occurrence, said: 'There are German soldiers in Joe's house, do you want to see them?' This statement was beyond our understanding. Why were they in Joe's house? Why were they in Ireland? Germany, we understood, was at war with other countries somewhere in the world but not in Ireland. Bewildered we got out of bed and went with Michael and my mother into Joe's kitchen. The following are my impressions of that night. I was 13, Michael 15 and Martha was 12.

On the cliff-top, not far from the white-washed walls which surround the lighthouse at Galley Head, West Cork, stands a roofless small hut. This is what remains of a concrete lookout post and is one of many which were constructed on the coastline around Ireland in the 1940s.

Men who knew the cliffs, inlets and shores of each particular place underwent a period of training and performed their duties, two at a time, day and night, as Coast Watchers. The hut had a telephone.

The assistant keeper at Galley Head was Joe O' Byrne who lived beside us with his wife and baby daughter. A third building called "The Spare House" was alongside Joe's. A telephone was located there as well.

On the night of March 13th 1945, all of us, except my father, went to bed. He said, "I will stay here in the kitchen for a short while." That puzzled me as he was not on duty. Joe had lit the lantern at sunset and he would keep watch until sunrise. The man on duty stayed in a room in the tower or in his kitchen where the range was always lighting.

Sometime after we went to sleep a loud explosion woke us and our bedroom was flooded with a pink light. My mother came to reassure us. There was a second loud bang and more pink light. We were alarmed for a while but quietness ensued and we went back to sleep. Our second disturbance was my father telling us about the soldiers. Of course, we wanted to see them.

We rushed to Joe's kitchen where we saw my father and Joe with five or six young men in uniform. The strangers were talking cheerfully together and did not have guns. From his experiences during World War 1 my father had a smattering of French and German, which enabled rudimentary conversation to take place. Soon afterward a Coast Watcher came with more uniformed Germans, making a total of eleven. All were happy to see each other. Joe's baby was brought in to be admired by the soldiers. One was their captain, according to my mother, and had children in his home country. They had scuttled their submarine U260 and made their way to the cliffs in a rubber dinghy. The pink light we had earlier seen was from flares set off by them.

"Which cliff?" I asked, since I had explored many of them being an agile cliff climber. My father said he did not know but I suspect he did. How did they manage to get safely up the cliffs? Their uniforms, as far as I could tell, were not wet with seawater.

We took a great interest in the discussion as to what food to give them. Tea was rationed and very precious. It was decided to give them coffee because they were 'from the continent' and were accustomed to that and not to tea. Ground coffee was not available. Irel coffee was made with boiling water added to the sweet syrupy essence. What food they were given I cannot remember. The "Cork Examiner" with EIRE printed on it was shown to them and they were delighted. The men knew Ireland was neutral.

All the while my mother and the three of us were observing and enjoying the excitement. Either my father, or Joe or a Coast Watcher, telephoned the authorities somewhere to inform them of the situation. There were procedures to be followed in an event like this at the Galley; there had been similar instances in other parts of Ireland.

At sunrise a member of either the LDF (Local Defence Force) or LSF (Local Security Force) from Clonakilty, with perhaps a Garda Siochana, arrived in a small lorry. They had come to take these sailors or soldiers to the Curragh Camp where they would be interned until the war was over. They were happy as they left Joe's house. They gave us cigarette tobacco, much appreciated by my father, odd tasting white chocolate, and pemmican, a dried, powdered beef that also tasted strange. Joe gave us the paddle, or oar, which the men had used. I have it still.

This I will always remember: as they were walking towards the lorry a soldier noticed a young woman who had come from the village with the local men to see "what was happening on the headland". He gave a flirty skipping dance towards her and went away in the lorry. I never knew any of their names.

We went to school that morning with our friends and talked about all that had happened. In school Master Griffin asked me to stand up and tell him the story. I was completely tongue-tied and could only think he should be asking Michael, who was older than me and would know what to say. Somehow or other he got the information by question and answer and to my great relief that was the end of it. When we got home from school we were told more men from the same U-Boat had been picked up off the coast. Michael and I later found a small white silk parachute on the cliff. We decided it was from one of the flares.

The U-Boat is at the bottom of the sea. Divers have been down to explore the wreckage. All I can think of is how dark and eerie it must be to travel under the sea in a U-Boat.

Two months later the war in Europe ended. It had been going very badly for Germany towards the end. Were the men in the U-Boat aware of this? If they were seamen, and not soldiers as my father described them, they would have known they were in neutral Irish waters. Did they scuttle the vessel to avoid further involvement in the war? On a small circle of paper in my mother's handwriting is the following: 'March 13th, 1945 German crew ashore from U Boat. 11 in all'.

Peggy

The local doctor assisted my birth at home in the 1940's. My father was a Garda so we had a good standard of living and a comfortable house with a garden that provided much of our food needs. We had a vegetable plot, apple trees, a variety of fruit bushes, hens, turkeys for Christmas, and our own cow; all tended by our busy parents.

I was the youngest of nine children and my eldest sister was 14 years older than me. As soon as she got home from high school each day she was told, "Get the child up and changed", and I was then her responsibility to mind. I went everywhere with her. Even when she was courting I was on the back of her bicycle when she and her boyfriend rode to Inchydoney Beach together. Eventually her wedding day arrived when I was 10 years old. It was a big shock to me to find I wasn't going on the honeymoon too! I just couldn't understand it.

My parents worked hard to ensure we all had a high school education. However, my father retired when I was ten, before we younger ones got through secondary school. My mother started up a bakery in a covered porch area at the back of our house, rising at 4am to make bread and cakes for the town in order to pay for our education, as secondary school was not free until 1966. My job was to deliver the finished goods to the shopkeepers during lunchtime. How I disliked that job! But, I am so grateful to my mother for the education I received.

I was reared with fear: fear of God and fear of authority, both at home and at school. Primary school was a happy time and I got on well there. But I didn't like secondary too much and there was huge fear there as well. If you did something wrong at school you got slapped and if your parents knew about it, you got slapped at home too.

The biggest highlight of summer was the Clonakilty Show. Crowds of people thronged down McCurtain Hill from the railway station through the town, to the Show Grounds, all generating a wonderful holiday atmosphere in the streets. My mother entered the Show cooking competitions and we were all pleased and proud of her, as she always did well in them.

There were loads of children in our street, so many that we had no need to go around the corner to make friends. We spent happy times playing 'Picky' (sometimes known as hop-scotch) with a stone and chalked lines on the street. We had skipping ropes and tops as well as playing tag.

When I was old enough to socialise at 17, we went to functions in the Industrial Hall. We were all expected to go straight home afterwards. However, there was always the temptation of having a quick cuddle with a favourite boy in a shop doorway en route. Woe betide those seen by the priest who never seemed to sleep at night. The congregation would be told at Sunday Mass of the depravity of the young people in the town. The guilt if you knew he had identified you was enormous, even though he never said your name. So, it was always a very short and nervous cuddle with one eye out for his approaching car.

After my father died when I was nineteen my mother gave me a small silver ring, very similar to a Claddagh ring, but without the crown above the heart. On the heart, held between two exquisitely made hands, were etched her initials. It was beautiful and finely made. She explained that my father had made it when he was a political prisoner on Spike Island, in Cork Harbour. Visitors used to smuggle small items into the prison in their shoes or socks. In this case a silver English sixpence had made its way to him and he had painstakingly fashioned it into this ring for his sweetheart. It was the first time I had seen the ring and heard its story. You can see the original sides of the sixpence on the inside of the ring.

Hannah

A neighbour and midwife were in attendance at my premature birth at home in the late nineteen thirties. We lived three miles from the centre of town and walked to church and school, sometimes getting a lift in the neighbour's horse and trap.

We didn't have umbrellas then. Our clothing consisted of coats, dresses, skirts and shoes or boots. The latter were obtained with assistance from a government subsidy that was available for the purchase of rough lace-up hobnail boots. Clothing and shoes were paid for weekly via account books at the drapers, with egg money from the hens. Schoolbooks were brought second hand, but we had new copy books.

We ate bread, butter and jam for lunch and for our dinner had vegetables with fry or stews, bacon or chicken. Milk puddings were made from bread and butter, rice or macaroni and we had blackberry, rhubarb or apple tarts all made by our mother. Hot cocoa drinks were a special treat. Our drinking water was drawn from the well.

We children helped out by the doing the washing up and small chores for our parents like going to town for messages, going for Woodbine cigarettes, taking the turkeys and goats to be mated, milking the goats, getting milk from our neighbour, catching the donkey for a trip to town, going to the river for a barrel of water for washing, taking the cart wheels to the river to tighten the rims, and picking blackberries and mushrooms.

For fun, I played with my sister, my cousin and the neighbours. Favourite games were playing shops, climbing trees, blind man's bluff, rolling hoops (old bicycle wheels) and we had swings in the hay sheds. We went to the river to swim, paddle and catch fish in jam jars. Sometimes we went to the seaside on foot, or in the donkey cart, where we paddled and had picnics. Indoors we played cards and board games. We loved it when the Fun Fair came to town.

In the 1930's and 40's during the World War 2 years we had an aunt and cousins from England sheltering and sharing our house with us. Following primary school I attended Sacred Heart Secondary School[20] and left with my Leaving Certificate in the mid 1950's. Although Secondary education was not free in those days, there were allowances made for students from less affluent families and as long as you paid something, and did your best at school, you could continue your education.

My first job was in the Farm Products chicken hatchery on Casement St. They collected eggs from all the different breeds and after hatching, sold them as day old chicks. I think there could have been up to 30 people working there at any one time. Following that I worked for a short time relieving a sick teacher in the primary school. While my Leaving Cert. marks did not qualify me for entry to Teacher's Training College, I did do well enough to achieve the Junior Assistant Mistress qualification that was then part of the Leaving Certificate.

In 1958 three of us girls, left for England to begin our nursing training at Croyden. My sister was already there. Those years were a grand time for us all, as there were loads of Irish in London.

****

---

[20] Registered as a Secondary School in 1941

Jean Crowley

My father was born in Casement Street, Clonakilty and my mother was from The Rock, Ringaskiddy on Cork Harbour. My mother had to leave school due to her mother's health at the age of 13, when her family moved to Grancore about 3 miles north, as the crow flies, of the Fernhill Hotel in Clonakilty. My grandmother suffered from asthma and my mother had to give her injections twice a day, as inhalers were not available then. She was the eldest daughter and had a hard life during her childhood. Being a bright child, she always felt a bit put out by having to leave school so early.

My parents met at a dance at the Show Grounds in Clonakilty. My father was a very well-known and well-liked salesperson who worked for Houlihan's Bakery. He drove a bread delivery van over quite a wide area of West Cork and was kind and obliging when it came to delivering letters and parcels for people along his route. After marriage, it was unusual in that he moved into my mother's home at Grancore. My granny had died some years earlier but grandad was still alive. He lived to a very great age, his early nineties, considering he had worked hard on the farm all his life, with horses and growing potatoes. There were 11 acres of land in small fields at Grancore including an apple orchard. Over time our family grew to three children, my older sister by three years, my younger brother and me the middle child born in the late 1950's.

My mother was a capable woman and very house-proud. She loved her clothes and kept herself well. She was also an excellent knitter and always had something on the needles. By knitting Aran pattern woollen garments for sale to American tourists and selling eggs from the hens she kept, she made herself an income. She taught us to save by giving us moneyboxes that could only be opened by can openers, which she kept under lock and key. "If you want something and you can't afford it, do it yourself", was another code she lived by. I remember watching her laying the carpet on our stairs herself.

The happy days of my childhood at home had a regular rhythm to them. Although Daddy was a country boy at heart, he would leave the house for work by 6am. Monday was always washday and my mother used a big metal bath to launder the clothes. The hot water was heated on a primus. The clothes were fed through the rollers of a mangle to wring them out. An aunty living in Shannonvale came to help with the laundry on her High Nellie[21] bicycle and did her own at same time. On Tuesdays the clean, dry clothes were ironed including starching all the shirt collars. Wednesday was the day for housework and the washing of windows. On Thursdays the house would be full of the smell of baking: the big farmhouse fruit cake made with butter sugar and eggs, the breads including currant bread baked the old fashioned way in the bastible. Friday was the day my mother went to town. She never learned how to drive our Morris Minor, possibly because Dad was an impatient teacher, so she often cycled in. On her return, the bike would be laden with two big shopping bags containing groceries, sewing and knitting supplies. On Saturday, she cleaned all the shoes, and polished all the woodwork with lavender scented wax, helped by my older sister Margaret. When that was completed she prepared the trifle and apple tarts for Sunday dinner.

On Sunday, we all went to 10 o'clock Mass in our Sunday best, and then home to a delicious hot meal after which Dad would usually take us for a spin to Glandore and Union Hall to show us off to his customers.

---

[21] Irish name for a ladies' bicycle on which one sits very upright.

Dancing became something very important in my life thanks to being taught at a young age by Mum and Dad and the three Kingston women who were friends of the family. The Bennett's, a Protestant family who lived next door, were wonderful neighbours to us being generous and thoughtful. They kept cows, pigs, sheep and a bull on their farm. On Saturdays, their house was always filled with the aroma of cooking. Mrs Bennett was an amazing baker and maker of crab-apple jelly, gooseberry, plum and blackberry jams. When we visited we always went away with mint caramel squares and cream cakes of every description. Mrs Bennett was also a nurse and when we were sick she was our first port of call.

We had a field that went down to the Argideen River and if there were no cattle in it we had summer picnics and played there. I particularly remember a birthday party where a picnic rug was spread out and we feasted on jam sandwiches, Marietta biscuits, cakes, and Krispie buns. The Bennet girls showed us how to make Top Hats. They were a Marietta biscuit topped with cooking chocolate with a marshmallow placed on top crowned by a Smartie, or other sweet, stuck on with more chocolate.

My sister and mother had a very close relationship, while I was closer to my father and brother. Daddy was a lovely man: he always called me Jeannie-wan. He never physically punished me. The rustle of the newspaper and the look he gave when he lowered it was enough to let me know I was out of order. On Friday nights Daddy would come home about 7.30pm often laden with treats; chocolate and coffee Swiss rolls, chocolate logs and fruit brack that would last us ten days. Sometimes we also had ice cream and Crunchy bars.

People didn't go to each other's houses in those days unless arrangements had been made. One day I set off on a bicycle ride and visited a friend in her home. On my return, I was told that it was totally unacceptable to go visiting someone at home without an invitation. My parents were also worried about the dangers of me being a young girl alone out in the countryside and were cross with me for that too.

I attended Knockskeagh School for my early education. By the age of thirteen I was travelling on the bus to Sacred Heart Secondary school daily in my dark green gym-slip with my older sister. The Principal of the school, Sister Benedicta, was very kind to me. I was just under 18 when I left after completing the Leaving Cert. Over the three months of summer school holidays I worked in housekeeping at Dunmore House Hotel. I lived in the chalets at the hotel and had a lot of fun. When off duty I used to hang out in the busy kitchen and help out. Sometimes we got a spin in to town with the people who holidayed at the hotel, to go to a dance. We had to find our own way back to Dunmore though. It can be a very long way when you are wearing the latest fashion clogs!

Macra na Feirme[22] was a marvellous organisation which made a huge difference to my social life at the time. It was one of the few clubs for young people. They offered all sorts of activities; like debating, bus trips away to Lisdoonvarna, public speaking, competitions in modelling clothing for particular occasions, flower arranging, cattle judging, and field days at other local clubs from Clonakilty to Millstreet. I loved conversation and getting to know people and I have kept those friendships alive to this present day.

After the holidays, I competed a commercial course at the Technical School in Clonakilty. I learned touch-typing, Dictaphone, commerce, and shorthand. I remember that the latter was handy to keep my diaries private from the

---

[22] An Irish voluntary rural youth organisation.

curious eyes of my sister. Following this I was employed on trial by Vincent Bennett (unrelated to our neighbours) in his supermarket on Pearse Street. He made a job for me and I loved working there. He was a fantastic boss and generous to his staff, with bonuses and Christmas parties. I still wear a very pretty ring I bought with money from a Christmas bonus one year.

My sister and I used to take turns to ask Daddy if we could borrow his car to drive in to the local dances. We always parked it a good distance from the venue because we felt that the old Morris Minor was a little embarrassing and not very stylish. We loved to dance to Elvis Presley, Cliff Richard, the Everley Brothers and the Beatles.

When I was 23 I went to Ostend in Belgium on holiday. My friend and I went to a ball there, where we felt very looked down upon by the other girls when they heard our Irish accents. There was a competition for the prize of Miss British Ball and I won it. The biggest prize was seeing the looks on those girls' faces!

I was married but it didn't work out. Now my daughters are older I am free to please myself with line and salsa dancing, cycling and Macra na Feirme. Like my mother I enjoy nice clothes and shoes and love to shop. Working at the supermarket adds interest to my life as I love interacting with people. It is nice to treat people, as you like to be treated yourself.

****

Woodfield Days

Although I did not come to live in the Clonakilty area until 1974, we frequently had summer holidays with relatives at Woodfield in the early 1950's. I loved staying there, it was such a novelty to be without electricity and to draw water from a well. Never did water taste so good as that delicious well water. Going out into the fields each day was also pure pleasure.

Our Woodfield family grew linen flax, one of oldest crops still cultivated in the world. Linen fabric has been made from flax since ancient times and the many by-products from its manufacture, such as seed, oil and tow, have been used in a multitude of ways over the centuries. It is a very labour-intensive crop that called on every member of the family, plus the neighbours, to assist in many of the steps. In addition, the women had to produce large quantities of food to nourish the workers. The production of linen in the West Cork area waxed and waned over the centuries due to economic factors. However, World War 2 shortages stimulated the industry again from 1941 to the mid 1950's.

The flax seed (linseed) was planted in the spring when the danger of frost had passed after preparing the soil in a way similar to that required if oats or barley were to be planted. After about three months growth, which included a period when its blue (or white) flowers bloomed, the flax was harvested. Before the linen seed was fully formed each plant had to be pulled up by the roots to avoid damaging the long flax fibres. They were then tied in bundles with binders made from specially prepared rushes. The next step involved the bundles of flax being immersed in carefully constructed ponds of water for some weeks to allow bacteria to assist in loosening the fibres from the stalks, a process called "retting". When retting was completed the air was filled with an awful stench. The resulting product was then lifted out and spread over the fields to dry. This was back breaking, dirty and often painful work as the woody stems were rough and sharp. Depending on the weather, when dry, the flax would be loaded up and taken by horse and cart to the Flax Mill at Lisavaird for scutching, a process where machinery would break the woody stems to release the long linen fibres. Scutching by-products produced were tow (the short linen fibres) and the woody bits, which were called showells or shous. The clean fine linen fibre would be baled and taken to Clonakilty to be sold to the representatives of the linen mills in the north at the Flax Market. [23]

The shous were a useful fuel source in times of shortage. However, my aunt used to pile them on top of the bastible when baking brown bread. She would light them and they quickly blazed up and died providing a short burst of heat to create a most delicious dark crust. When we visited the mill we children used to gather up any tow lying about and bring it home. There we would find an old bottle with a cork, then jam the tow into the neck to make a doll with "real" hair. The tow could hold in any number of fancy hairstyles and even be curled and keep its shape.

As well as happy memories, I also have a piece of history from Woodfield, a sampler that came to me as a grand-niece of General Michael Collins [24]. The sampler was stitched by his mother, Mary Anne O'Brien, and is believed to be on family produced linen. On the day that the British Army were burning down the family home, my Great Uncle, Liam Collins, was a baby who had been taken outside in his cradle. The soldiers snatched the cradle from

---

[23] see p.16 of The Ardfiedl/Rathbarry Journal 1998-99 for a detailed article.
[24] The Irish Revolutionary Leader, born Woodfield, 1890-1922. Statue P98.

the baby and flung the cradle on the flames too. The sampler was one of the few things that survived the fire because it had been tied into a bundle and thrown from an upstairs window.

Many years later the sampler went to my grandmother in Cork. Maeve, my youngest aunt, found it and had it framed. My grand-mother wrote on the back of the sampler, 'For my daughter, Maeve'. Later when Maeve joined a religious order she gave it to me, writing a similar inscription on the back, thus giving the back of the framed sampler a written history all of its own.

****

Ann O'Leary

We were a farming family living in the Barryroe area. But despite growing up on a farm, I know very little about farming and have never seen an animal born. This was because farming was considered "men's work" and we women and girls were concerned mainly with the house. This was not just the view of my family but of the majority of farming families at the time. I was born in 1968 and became the middle child of five children. I had two older brothers and one younger. My sister was the baby of the family. My father was a mixed farmer with tillage and dairy cows. I never knew, and still don't know how many cattle we had or how many acres we owned. Once I asked my father these questions as our teacher had given them as homework. His answer was, "We have a lot of land when the tide goes out". That is all he would say. When on the rare occasion I did take an interest in what was happening on the farm, I was told, "Go into the kitchen and make an apple tart".

To begin with, a horse and cart took our milk to the creamery. Later, a tractor and trailer replaced this. The cows were milked in the stall (milking parlour) with an electric . This consisted of a pipeline that sucked the cow's teats into the clusters of cups, and then in a pulsating motion sucked the milk from the cow into a bucket. The bucket was then lifted and poured into the churn. When he returned from the creamery Dad would bring about six churns out onto the milk stand, which was at the same height as the horse and cart. It was women's work to clean the empty churns and we girls did that. We had to put our arms and hands inside them and scrub them out with Vim abrasive powder. No rubber gloves for us. Then we rinsed the churns with water from buckets under the drainpipes that collected roof water in the stall. When the bulk tank was installed, instead of the milk being poured into the churns it was poured from the buckets into the tank. Thus, there were no churns to wash anymore, because twice daily the milker rinsed the milk tank.

It was also our job to feed the hens and collect the eggs from the hen house. The hens were kept for egg supply to the home only. It was my mother's hot and dirty task to clean out the hen house.

There was a lot of segregation of men and women when I grew up. When someone died in the district and a wake was held, the women congregated in the kitchen or beside the coffin. The men all sat together in the best room, the parlour, which was only used for the Stations and Christmas celebrations. Wherever the men gathered there was always "a drop to drink", in other words alcohol. Tea was for the women. At the graveyard, prior to the burial taking place, there was a tradition of offering every male "a drop" as he entered. I saw this myself. On each support of the graveyard gate stood a bottle of whisky with a glass beside it. The men on each side of the gate filled the glass for each passing male. Nothing was offered to the women.

"The Stations" was a gathering where the local townland would be invited to a house for the celebration of Mass. This occurred roughly once every seven years as each house took its turn in rotation. While the men all sat in the parlour with the priest, the women were in the kitchen preparing and serving food. Preparation for the Stations would have begun weeks before with everything in the house and yard made spic and span and sufficient ware (plates, cups and glasses) and chairs borrowed from the neighbours to cope.

In our townland, the Stations were never held on a Sunday. They were held at either noon or 8pm any day bar Saturday or Sunday. Before the Mass the priest would hear confessions in the parlour from anyone who wanted it. Then he would celebrate the Mass. Members of the family of the house would be involved by reading from the Bible or saying a prayer. The priest would then ask how many people were for communion today. He would count out the host[25] according to the number of hands raised. When the Mass was over he would pray for the dead of the townland and then collect the station dues. When he called out each family name in turn, the man of the house would give him an envelope containing an offering of money. All the families present made these offerings to the Priest, including the hosting family. The priest would then announce who was to hold the next Stations, and go to the parlour and sit with the men.

The usual procedure was then to offer a meal which in later times became a salad plate: boiled eggs, two types of cold meat, potato salad, coleslaw, lettuce, sliced onions, tomatoes, and beetroot. This would be served with sliced white pan[26], home-cooked brown soda bread and tea. A dessert feast would follow. Usually two types: apple tart and sherry trifle plus laden tiered cake-stands with slices of porter cake, and buns of all descriptions. When the table was finally cleared everyone would be asked, "What would you like to drink?" On offer were: whiskey, brandy, port, Baileys Irish Cream, sherry and more recently wine for the ladies. It wasn't uncommon for 8pm Stations to last until 4am. In later years some households moved to midday Stations, where being mid-week, they would mainly be attended by women and thus were easier to manage.

Our kitchen had a concrete floor and against one wall a settle was placed. It could be used for an extra bed, but we used it instead to store shoes, boots and trainers. We

---

[25] Consecrated bread
[26] A shop bought loaf of white bread, raised with yeast.

children sat on the settle for meals. The kitchen table was pushed up against it. In the mornings, there would be no fire in the kitchen to warm it, and so we used a Superser gas heater to take the chill away. Our school clothes were aired on it until they were warm, before we got into them. It could also be used to make toast. There was a back kitchen where all the cooking was done. It was a small two storied addition to the house and the upper floor was a grain store reached by a set of stairs on the outside. In our house, in common with most of our neighbours, the eggs and tea kettle were boiled on a primus stove. Toast was also made on the poker over the coal fire. Never did toast taste so delicious!

My mother was a wonderful cook, but she did not use recipe books. Everything was done from memory. As we had no scales everything was a fist of this and a pinch of that. She baked all our bread in a gas oven. Breads were brown or white soda cakes she shaped in a round and marked with a cross and a dimple in the centre of each quarter. Tea brack was made with tea and dried fruit and curranty cake was one of our favourites (a white soda bread with currants in it). A very modern electric fan oven was bought when I was in secondary school in the early 1970's. However, my mother always regretted it, as it didn't do as good a job as the gas one.

On the rare occasions we bought a sliced pan, it came from Houlihan's Bakery in Clonakilty. It could be brought directly from the bakery, on the corner by the "Wheel of Fortune Pump", or from Houlihan's shop on Ashe Street, facing the statue of Tadhg an Asna, on Asna Square. When you purchased the bread, they wrapped it especially for you in crisp white paper. Barm brack was made at Halloween. Traditionally the barm brack contained a pea, a rag, a stick, a small coin and a ring. If you received a slice with one of the objects in it, the superstitious meaning applied to you:

the pea meant you would not marry that year; the rag would mean bad luck or poverty; the stick would mean an unhappy marriage or fighting; the coin would mean riches; and the ring, the most desired outcome by girls, would mean you would marry, possibly within the year.

At home, we had our breakfast about 8am, at 10am we had tea, and 1pm was the time for the main hot dinner of meat and vegetables. At 4pm a cup of tea would be served with a slice of cake or bun. On Friday, dinner was always fish, generally delicious smoked haddock in a stew with peeled potatoes, carrots, onions and white sauce. When my father and brothers were out working in the fields at break time, tea and bread, or brack, would be taken out to them. My mother poured the tea with milk and sugar into a clean, glass Deasy's mineral bottle and stopped it with a cork. This would be placed in a thick knitted sock to keep it warm and I would pedal out to the fields with it on the carrier of my bike. Before rubber hot water bottles became the norm, this corked bottle of hot water in a sock was a good way of warming chilly feet too.

Every Friday my sister and I had to collect the men's soiled clothing from their bedrooms. We washed it in a Hoover Twin Tub machine, in the evening. Although it washed and spun the clothes all by itself, you still had to lift them from the wash compartment into the spin one. In contrast to the modern fully automatic machines you could control the wash time and spin time yourself, which in some ways was more convenient. The laundry was then put up on the fireguard in front of the coal fire. If Saturday was a dry day we hung it out on a long double clothesline my father made. Once pegged out a clothes prop was used to raise the line into the breeze.

On Saturday night, the girls' job was to apply shoe polish to all the men's black shoes and buff them to a brilliant shine with newspaper. Ironing of the dry clothes

was also expected. Our old iron (pictured above) required the separate stone to be put in the fire to be heated and then it was placed inside a little door above the iron plate. However, an electric iron replaced it eventually, but it still required some clothes to be sprinkled with water first.

We all took our weekly bath one after the other on Saturday to be looking our best for Mass. I often wished to wash more often but hot water seemed to be in short supply and it couldn't be wasted. If we behaved well at Sunday Mass and didn't turn around to look behind us (which showed disrespect) we would be allowed a treat: a shop-bought, thick block of ice-cream sliced from a brick and placed between two crispy wafers. Mmmm. Another treat we sometimes enjoyed was a lemonade or an orange mineral [27], the only two flavours available. When we returned the bottle to the shop we got five pence back, which we then spent on sweets ; like bullseyes, boiled sweets or my favourite glucose sweets. Sweets were usually weighed out from tall glass jars in grocery shops.

---

[27] Non-alcoholic carbonated drink.

A lesson that has stayed with me since my childhood is that looking in a mirror was vanity, and vanity is a sin. To this day I feel uncomfortable looking in a mirror especially at the hairdressers, when conversation is often carried out with the hairdresser standing behind me, while we look at each other in the mirror.

As I grew older I realised that my family were lucky enough to have some things at home that others lacked. We were amongst the first in our area to get a flush toilet in the outhouse, a car, a coin-operated telephone in the house and a television set. The neighbours used to come in and watch TV with us. My father, who was very good with his hands, came up with a clever contraption so that the TV could be neatly concealed at a moment's notice and look exactly like a nice cabinet. Dad collected our groceries from the Barryroe Co-op in the car. When I was older I sometimes bought them back on my bike, one bag on each handlebar and one on the carrier.

When I was 14 years old I was taken from school for a whole year to take care of and help my mother who had been very ill. I learnt a lot about running an orderly household in that time. Once my mother was in better health I wanted to go back and resume my schooling, because I was tired of having to be the "mother" of the house. I also knew that if I didn't go back to school, I would probably be at home for the rest of my life. My brothers used to go in to the dance in "The Lilac" in Enniskeane when I was a teenager. I begged to be allowed to go along with them. My father refused to let me go, saying, "No you are a girl and you can't do what the men do".

By all accounts my mother was a beautiful young woman. She married a farmer whose mother was very poorly, and didn't have anyone to care for her. So, as a new bride she cooked and cleaned for her husband, her sick mother–in-law and farm helpers. All her life she has been generous and unsparing of herself in terms of taking in and caring for others including our long-term farm worker. He came to us a stranger and lived upstairs with us until his death about 40 years later. He was a good worker and a lovely man with never a bad word to say of anyone. When my father died he said, "God should have taken me". My father was a kind and helpful person. He was very good mechanically and could fix anything. One day he stopped on the road to fix a breakdown on a stranger's car. The owner asked my father what he owed him. Dad said, "Nothing, but if you could put me in touch with a young man looking for farm work, I would be glad of it." The stranger worked in a hospital and knew someone who would make a good farm worker, and that is how our worker came to us.

****

Pauline Lowney

Mill House, Ballinascarthy was the place I called home from the beginning of my life in the late 1940's. The local nurse delivered me and suggested (as they often liked to do) that my mother name me Rose, because June was the month of roses. But instead my mother chose my name to commemorate the Feast Day of St Peter and St Paul.

The railway line ran across the bottom of our garden and from the station in the village we could travel to Cork or Clonakilty, or via a side line to Courtmacsherry. We loved to watch Dan, the train guard, wave his red flag to signal to the driver that all were aboard, before he quickly hopped into his van at the end of the train. Then there would be a puff of steam from the engine and off the train would go. My mother drove us in the family Ford Prefect car to the convent school in Clonakilty each day, but sometimes if she couldn't collect us, we went home on the train. It took about 15 minutes to arrive at our station. Each year for a special treat we also took the train over to Courtmacsherry for the regatta. Watching the local rowing teams compete, eating ice-cream and meeting friends was a big part of it. Amusements like swing boats and bumper cars were added fun.

Our home farm had dairy cows, poultry and sows with their annual litter of bonhams[28]. I think the neighbours provided the boar, as was common then. My best friend used to have to load the family hen-turkey into the pram and take it to the neighbouring farm at mating time. We girls never saw anything of the actual mating act, we would be banished to the house while it was going on.

On our farm, we were self-sufficient in most things required for a healthy diet. My parents always did the

---

[28] Piglets

milking; they were very particular about it being done carefully as it was all done by hand. They made a very good team working together on many aspects of farm life. From about the age of ten, one of my responsibilities was to bring the cows in from the pasture a little way down the quiet country road. Our sheep dog and a stick were all I needed to carry out this pleasant chore. Carrying water was another job to be done. All the water for the washing associated with milking and cleaning down the yard afterwards was brought from the River Abha na Caoch (Blind River) a tributary of the Argidene. It was usually brought in buckets but sometimes a barrel on a horse drawn wagon was used. Water for household use was carried in buckets from the Ballinascarthy village pump. This was a chore I liked to avoid when I was a teenager and always asked my older sister to do, as I wasn't comfortable for some reason I still don't understand. Maybe it had something to do with all the village boys who congregated in the area there, yet I knew them all and wasn't shy, nor frightened by them.

We had a big vegetable garden growing potatoes, carrots, parsnips, turnips and onions. For jam, puddings and tarts we had rhubarb, gooseberry and currant bushes and apple trees. My mother was a marvellous cook and she turned all our home-grown food into delicious meals. We were very lucky in that we always had plenty of good food; stews, roast beef, chicken and ham, or chicken and boiling bacon. We had the occasional leg of lamb as a treat. We were unusual in that we had electricity in our house way before most people in our area did. It was because there was a disused mill on our property. As the millwheel was still working and close to the house, it was used to generate electricity from the running water. This gave us electric lighting and an electric stove for cooking which was somewhat rare. The stove had two round flat solid elements or plates and a big rectangular one at the front. Mother frequently made drop scones on this and the oven baked wonderful sponges, Madeira cakes, soda bread and rock buns. She taught us girls everything we needed to know about feeding a family and it stood us in good stead later.

We also had cooking classes at school, using recipes from the "All in the Cooking" book, which covered all the necessary basics required like soda bread. "Mrs Beeton's Book of Household Management" was also in our kitchen. Although first published in 1861, it was full of advice and had things to say about animal welfare and seasonal fresh produce that are still current today, as well as about 900 recipes[29]. We were taught to knit at school too, one project being a very complicated one: a stocking knitted using four needles. "Turning the heel" was the really hard part. I confess I cheated and asked my mother to do it for me. Luckily for me, knitting stockings and socks do not feature much in today's lifestyle. However, we did learn how to darn at home, but I never had much time for it as an adult. In second class, at about 8 or 9 years old, we were also taught to sew. We learned all the different stitches like top-stitch, running, buttonhole and hemming stitches using just a needle and thread and a piece of fabric.

Household chores were also part of life for us. The concrete kitchen floor needed to be scrubbed every Saturday with us down on our hands and knees with the scrubbing brush and bucket. We also had to scrub the underside of the wooden table where people rested their feet. We had no modern toilets but instead chamber pots under the beds that were emptied into a covered bucket that was placed on the landing. The covered bucket was then emptied onto the farmyard manure. The used pots

[29] https://en.wikipedia.org/wiki/Isabella_Beeton

were then taken to the river to clean and were scrubbed with gravel, until Vim powder cleanser became available. Laundry was also a big task. I can vividly remember my mother sitting alongside the Burco Boiler after the washing had been boiled, scrubbing at the spots before it was rinsed, wrung out by twisting it by hand and hung out on the clothesline. Later we had a rotary style washing machine complete with wringer. The heavy wet clothes had to be lifted up and fed through the rollers of the wringer to expel the water. All this hard work must have made our skin rough and sore, but I do not recall any soothing creams or lotions then. Much later we did appreciate a pot of Ponds Cold Cream[30] if we were lucky enough to have one.

The village creamery was the hub of Ballinascarthy then. The men gathered to swap stories as they delivered their farm produce and shopped for supplies. It stocked most of the articles we needed for life on the farm and was just a short walk away for us. Our poultry came to us as day old chicks, which we ordered by phone, one hundred chicks at a time from Cork Farm Products. We would go down to the village to collect them as they came in on the bus from Cork with all the passengers. They were cute little bundles of yellow fluff in cardboard boxes, which we took home and set under an infrared lamp to keep them warm. My mother raised them and killed and dressed them herself, two each time, for our dinners. There was only one phone in the village in my youth and it belonged to our obliging neighbours. When my baby brother was born that was how we heard the news, from a message sent via our neighbour's phone.

Popular sports at the time were trotting races and these are still sometimes held today. They were held on the roads

[30] First launched in 1907. http://www.pondsinstitute.co.uk/history.php

and the horses had mounted jockeys, instead of riders in sulkies harnessed behind the horse. The aim was to be the fastest to the finish, without breaking into a canter as that led to disqualification. Braking and turning the horse was a very skilled part of it. My father had a very fine trotting horse called Billy Boy, which he took to these races in a lorry. He also entered in the Clonakilty Show. The competition there was about how well the horses harnessed to gigs moved, the action of their legs and how well they worked. The night before my mother sat up late finishing off new clothes for us for show day. We girls all had ribbons in our hair and we loved sitting up in the beautiful wooden gig with Dad, as Billy Boy slowly trotted around the show ring.

Visiting our grandmother, Gaggy, was a pleasant activity we enjoyed. My mother's mother came from Bean Hill, near Shannonvale. We would set off on the two-mile walk from our home. My sisters were accompanied by their two pet hens, which liked to walk with them. While there we chatted with Gaggy while doing a bit of gardening, feeding the hens and turkeys and getting the guinea fowl out of the trees, where they liked to lodge. It was so enjoyable to walk the country roads and so quiet compared to today. As the years passed by I began to be allowed to go with my three older sisters to social events where other young people gathered. Locally there was a little hall for dancing and up by Pedlars Cross, a dancing platform in the open air. An accordion player usually provided both modern and traditional music and the dancing would vary between traditional and modern too, depending on the crowd. There was also modern dancing at the Industrial Hall in Clonakilty and in Enniskeane at the Lilac Ballroom. When I was 17 a boyfriend taught me how to drive and so I was allowed to use the family car to transport friends to dances with me. In our home, we had a large unused room that was often used for a grand night of singing and dancing after the threshing of crops or The Stations. My parents were very social people and donated land from our property for the siting of the Ballinascarthy Hall that stands today. I also attended groups especially for rural people; the Macra Na Feirme meetings for the young ones and sometimes went with my mother for tea and discussion at the ICA[31].

At sixteen years of age I left school and went to live-in at Dunmore House Hotel. One of my sisters had married into the family that ran the hotel. There I put my cooking skills learned from mother to good use. I was once asked how I knew when a piece of meat was cooked. For me it was just instinctive from the smell of the food and the feel and colour of the juices when it was prodded with a skewer. I later worked two summers at a hotel in Kenmare where I learned even more about the hospitality industry.

I was married in Clogagh Church and my wedding reception was held at Dunmore House. It is a beautiful venue with its views of Inchydoney and the sea. We left from there for a week's honeymoon in Majorca. On return I moved four miles into my husband's town of Clonakilty, where over the years we raised three of our own children and three of my sister's. It was here I got very involved in the hobby of water sports, especially water skiing, which we used to enjoy at Ring and Rosscarbery. Later I began a new career as a driver of mini-buses for schoolchildren and people with special needs.

Looking back, it seems to me that my life was rather ordinary but through it all I have always been and still am very busy and fully engaged with family, friends and community. Right now, I find great pleasure in my first grandchild, granddaughter Zoe, born in Jan 2015.

---

[31] Irish Countrywomen's Association

Clonakilty Bay

A West Cork Farmer's Wife

I am a Kerry woman and after leaving school in the early 1960's gained a clerical job in a bank. We worked from 9.30 am until 5 pm, although none could leave until the tellers had balanced the books, so occasionally it was later. In those times, all the senior positions were held by men and there was no way that a woman could advance above the position of clerk, nor achieve a cashier's position, no matter how good she was at the job. There was also no chance of working in your own hometown, you were transferred to wherever you were needed entirely at the bank's discretion. We were all happy to accept this because in those days we felt very fortunate to have any job at all and a bank job was excellent because it was secure.

Catholic social teaching, based on the belief that a woman's 'natural role' was as a wife and mother, heavily influenced early Government thinking. Women were expected to be 'modest, retiring and obedient'. In addition, it was considered that women working for pay were taking jobs from men with families to keep. This resulted in the introduction of the 1932 Public Service Marriage Bar[32]. Originally brought in to cover teachers, it spread to nurses and many other occupations. While working in the bank I met my future husband and on our marriage in 1967, I was thus dismissed from the bank and began my new role as a farmer's wife in the Clonakilty area.

In the late 1960's there were substantial numbers of educated women attracted to farm life. Agriculture was in an expansionist mode and farmers were doing well financially. The effect of rural electrification was starting

---

[32] The Marriage Bar was withdrawn in 1972. However, for teachers it was lifted in 1957.

to bring prosperity to the farming community through the use of milking machines and water pumps. Wives could see an outlet for the skills they had gained in their working lives, for example, through keeping the farm accounts. Often the business focus they brought to the job was an advantage to the profit side of farming. The women worked hard for the farm, doing all the cooking every day, feeding extra workers at harvest time, being available at a moment's notice to provide an extra pair of hands to assist with everyday farming tasks, as well as bringing up children and ensuring that they received a good education, plus keeping a good home.

However, due to the male focus on men's work being more important in those times, the PRSI contributions of the women were overlooked when many farmers and their accountants paid tax for future pensions. Thus, many women, now in their early 70's, after decades of record keeping and helping out with farm work, had to fight for the right to a state pension because the government had no record of them working for the minimum period required. A famous letter from a farmwife in the Irish Farmer's Journal[33] at the time stated that, "she, along with doing all the other jobs on the farm, had to stand in for Shep [34], when Shep was missing!" However, some accountants did pay the PRSI contribution as the wives were legally deemed to be partners in work and ownership.

The first time I stayed in the home of my future in-laws was after I became engaged. As I had been transferred miles north from Co. Cork with the bank, if I wanted to see my boyfriend, I had to stay with his cousins nearby. My mother and father-in-law, as was the common rural

---

[33] A weekly farm newspaper
[33] The dog.

custom, then lived with us for the first decade or more of our marriage. They had been late marrying, as they had to wait until the Civil War of 1922-1923 was over, because they had been on different sides. The history of 600 years of English oppression, the War of Independence from 1919-1921 and the Civil War have had a huge impact on the psyche of the Irish people. People became very cute (cagey) and kept their business and thoughts to themselves. This persisted until fairly recent times with, for example, farmers keeping their acreage, and stock numbers closely guarded.

Another huge historic impact on the fortunes of the agricultural community was known as the Economic War, or Anglo-Irish Trade War, which came after the fight for freedom and Civil War and lasted from 1932 until 1938. It came about because De Valera's government refused to honour provisions made in the 1921 Anglo-Irish Treaty for land annuities to be paid to Britain[35]. The result was a protectionist trade war with unilateral trade barriers imposed by both sides that resulted in Irish farmers losing the market for much of their production. The knock-on effects were severe social suffering and financial loss for Ireland. Eventually measures were instituted to offset this, such as making Irish Cattle and British Coal cheaper and easier to purchase, and this eventually gave rise to the Anglo-Irish Trade agreement that effectively brought about the end of the trade war three years later. However, these extremely difficult times left a long legacy of deprivation, for farmers and their families in particular, to cope with.

---

[35] The Irish Lands Act 1870 had enabled some Irish tenant farmers to buy their own lands with the help of British loans, which were to be repaid by annuities.

Macra na Feirme, a network of clubs was founded in 1944 by a group of 12 agricultural advisors, rural science teachers and farmers with the aim of helping the personal development of young rural people. It provides training and experience in many aspects of farming, communication and social abilities and has since made a big contribution to country life for those aged between 17 and 35, both male and female.

I think that Mary Robinson[36] our first female President of Ireland from 1990 to 1997 was also a huge positive influence for the women of Ireland. As a strong independent woman, an academic and barrister, combined with good looks, a husband and family, she drew a large following with her championing of women's rights.

Former Taoiseach[37] Charles Haughey, although now a controversial figure, in the course of his long career also brought about beneficial changes to the laws affecting women, such as: family planning, legitimacy of children, discrimination against women in inheritance rights, free secondary education and also put in place free transport and electricity for old age pensioners. He also effectively abolished the death penalty and supported the arts by giving tax free status to writers and artists and making books VAT free.

[36] Elected directly by the people she served two seven year terms as President and then five years as the United Nations High Commissioner for Human Rights.
[36] Prime Minister

The "Wheel of Fortune" water pump on Connolly Street. One of the main sources of water for Clonakilty town until electricity came in the 1950's.

Dublin was where I was born and raised. Following Art College, I tried to get a job/apprenticeship in one of the very few potteries in Ireland but there were no openings at the time. I got the UK directory of potters and wrote to a selection of them. I received a few offers and opted to take up the offer of work in the Alderney pottery as I have always had a grá [38] for islands.

It was there that I met Jim who was also working in the pottery. We decided that we would really like to open our own pottery and came to look in West Cork for an affordable property. I had visited West Cork as a student when I spent a few weeks as an au pair for a family on holidays in Glandore and had loved it. Jim suggested it would be a good compromise as it was half way between Cornwall and Dublin, our respective places of birth. We didn't find any suitable place on our first visit and returned to Alderney where we showed friends the property details we had taken back with us. They were impressed by what was available and with the cheap prices so made the trip and found a house before we did! On our second trip the farmer who had sold the house to our friends told us about this old farm house which was derelict and we fell for it. I particularly loved the huge old elm trees in the garden and was heartbroken when, after a couple of years, we had to cut them down as they were diseased (Dutch elm disease) and rotten. Buying the house and land in Rossmore turned out to be complicated as the deeds were missing and the bank wanted the signature of the original owner who at this stage was well dead! We paid a deposit and left the paper work in the hands of the solicitor here and went off to work in other potteries. We had more or less written it

---

[38] love

off when four years later we got a letter from our solicitor saying the property was ours.

We were at this stage living in Cornwall and had just had a baby. But we packed everything up and moved with our six-month-old baby to start our adventure in West Cork in 1980.

The house was now a total ruin with the roof fallen in and windows fallen out! There was no water or electricity supply. We started life off here living in a tiny caravan on site. Jim did all the building work himself by hand and without the aid of electricity for the first year. Before we drilled the well we had to drive to the village with cans to collect our daily water from the pump there. My daughters are amazed when I tell them that I had to hand wash the baby's nappies outside in buckets before we had running water! This went on for over a year as it took months for the ESB to put in poles and then we were shocked to learn that we had to wait another year for a different team from another branch of the ESB to come and put in the wires and finally connect us up. We didn't have a telephone for the first few years and had to use the phone box in the village. It is amazing to think that there was a two-year waiting time in the 1980's to have a telephone installed in your home!

During this period Jim worked on the house, including making windows using hand tools and traditional wooden pegs to join the timbers of the A framed roof structure. He was very good at stonework and did some building stonework jobs for other people to bring some money in. I started a vegetable garden, with a lot of advice from our neighbour who instructed me in the art of planting and growing potatoes, as I had never grown them before. We planted as wide a range of vegetables as possible and eventually were self-sufficient in a wider variety of produce than found in the shops. I walked down to the village shop every day with the baby in the pram to buy our bread and milk and any groceries that we needed. Like most people we had a "book", that is a shop account, which was paid off monthly. The Post Office, which was part of the village shop, provided a great service and was a social meeting point until it closed a few years ago. Other things like hardware and building materials etc. came from the local creamery.

Our neighbours were mostly elderly bachelors who were friendly and welcoming, but probably viewed us as eccentric, or as they would have said then, "hippies". They lived simple traditional lives where they took their milk to the creamery with the horse and cart and cut the grass for hay by hand. I loved seeing all the little haystacks appearing every year. One of our neighbours was very happy that we had moved in, as he "liked to see new blood in the area". We seemed to be surrounded by bachelors, there was a shortage of women as many of them had emigrated to get work that was not available locally.

There were plenty of pubs around, but as we had practically no money we didn't go out much and here drinking was mainly a male pass-time. I met very few women in the local county pubs and was usually the only woman there.

After the first year here and running out of money we had to decide whether to finish the house, or use the money to build the pottery workshop, which is what we did. We had brought some equipment and a couple of pottery wheels with us from England, but Jim had to build a kiln, which was a big project. We got a small grant towards this and building the workshop from the local County Development Team and an expensive overdraft from the bank. We started by making earthenware flower pots along with parsley and strawberry pots and got our first order for these from Shanahan's Nursery in

Clonakilty. We then made down draft chimney pots, as there was a demand for these in Building Suppliers at the time. After that we progressed to making a range of table ware, initially selling to local craft shops and then to the Cork Craftsman's Guild shop in Cork. At this stage, we had had another baby so I was always juggling working and child minding and usually worked at night after they were asleep. We then showed our work at the National Craft Fair and got orders nationally.

In 1980 the Society of Cork Potters was formed in Bandon with potters attending from all over West Cork. It was a very supportive organisation with regular monthly meetings held in member's homes/studios. Everyone helped and encouraged one another. We would all bring food and drink to the meetings and make a party of it once business had been done. We challenged each other to make different "bigger and better" pieces through working for various exhibitions. In 1985 when Jim was the Chair, we wrote to Diane Feinstein who was the Mayor of San Francisco and she put us in contact with the California Association of Ceramic and Glass artists. Cork and San Francisco cities were twinned so we invited the California potters to Cork to exhibit with us in a joint Irish-American show at the Crawford Gallery in 1985. This was a great success and with support of the Crafts Council of Ireland we travelled the exhibition to Dublin. The following year a couple of the American potters came over to do a workshop with Cork Potters at Lettercollum House near Timoleague. The house was run as a hostel then and had plenty of space both in the house for the accommodation and plenty of barns to hold the workshops and to build kilns. There was always huge attendance from all over the country at these events, as there wasn't really any else like it in the rest of the country. Before we moved here a co-operative called the Craftsman's Guild Shop was established in Cork in the 1970's to sell the increasingly popular arts and crafts burgeoning in Ireland, like pottery, textiles, wood-turning, metalwork, baskets. It was through the Cork shop, which had changed and evolved, that we received our first orders for pottery tableware in 1984. It was so busy then that I remember delivering pottery a couple of days before Christmas day and people were grabbing it straight out of the boxes before it was even unwrapped! There was a huge interest in handmade crafts and even though VAT was very high at about 30%, we were doing well. Local people and many of the diaspora wanted locally made things to take back home or send abroad, particularly to the USA. A lot of the potters then were English who had moved to West Cork for a better way of life, but there were Irish potteries based at Cape Clear and Schull. There probably would have been as many women as men potters.

We had a good 20 years of wholesaling tableware and also making special one-off exhibition pieces and at the end of the 90's we could see change coming. Jim started teaching part time and I did a yearlong "Women in Business" course that was organized by the local Enterprise Board. We were considering what direction the pottery should take in the changing market place. We wanted to move away from the large wholesale productions we were doing and were looking at the possibility/viability of doing a website to sell on line, when suddenly an opportunity arose to have a partnership with another maker in a shop in Clonakilty to each sell our own products directly. I did this for a couple of years which gave us a feel for the local market and it was great to get direct feedback from customers which you don't get when you are wholesaling.

After a couple of years, we decided to go our separate ways. I then opened Etain Hickey collections in Ashe

Street, initially selling our own and other West Cork Art and Crafts but quickly realised I needed to supplement this with more giftware. In 2003 Clonakilty became Ireland's first Fair Trade town. I decided to go down the Fair Trade route and buy as much of this as I could. This had to be sourced in the UK where they have certified businesses (BAFTS) importing from India and other countries. Fair Trade is about better prices, decent working conditions and fair terms of trade for workers and support for community projects. I also feel that women benefit most as they get paid a fair equal wage. I love the Fair Trade products as they are all handmade, often quirky, and colourful. This fits in with my own ceramics, which tend to be very colourful too. There is a hidden wealth of talent in West Cork. So, from the start I have enjoyed inviting different artists and makers to exhibit their work in my annual exhibitions, thus visitors and locals alike can see some beautiful work that they might not otherwise be aware of. Looking back over the past 10 years I see that I have tended to show a lot more women artists and craft makers! There have been huge changes here in the past 40 years, but what has remained the same is the welcome, the friendliness and the openness to change in the people of West Cork.

Written by Etain herself.

****

An Educator

One of my early memories of Clonakilty as a child in the 1950's, was staying with my uncle a priest in Emmet Square on New Year's Eve. In bed at midnight I was startled to hear a loud bell ringing outside the window. Looking into the deserted Emmet Square I saw a man on the back of a lorry ringing a hand bell while being driven from street to street in the town to announce the New Year to everyone. It was so different from the celebrations of today.

My father was a hardworking, self-educated farmer who believed in the importance of a good education for all of his seven children. That is how I came to board in the Sacred Heart Secondary School in Clonakilty in the mid 1960's.

It was a tough regime in those days. School was based on the male model of control in society. We had to eat our breakfast in silence, as if silence would stop us thinking or interacting. We only went home for the school holidays. The rest of the time we were within the confines of the school save for walking to confession at the parish church on Saturdays and on Sundays going on long supervised exercise walks. Our lives were dominated by schoolwork, which embraced Saturday morning as well. In the evenings, we studied from 5pm to 7pm and broke for supper, then studied again from 7.30pm to 9.30pm, or 10pm, if important exams were looming. Sport and exercise were not catered for in a big way. We played netball amongst ourselves, and tennis if we were interested and had a racquet.

The lights went out at 10pm but most of us had torches. I ruined my eyesight reading under the blankets until all hours. It was a sad day when the batteries ran out because we Boarding School girls were forbidden from entering any of the shops in town and could not replace them until the holidays. There was a little sweet shop on Ashe Street that had a jukebox. We gave our town dwelling classmates money to play popular songs for us as we dawdled past on our way to confession and when we lingered outside on our way back. It was magic to hear Elvis, the Beatles or the Capital Showband this way.

On Sundays, we also wrote home to our parents who received the letter the following Tuesday. Our reply came the following Friday. It was by letter from school that I told my parents that I had decided on the life of a religious sister. It seemed a long wait to hear their response. Both were happy and not so happy about my decision, but they supported me in my choice. Most girls then went from school at 17 or 18 to begin their novitiate. At that time, anyone who wanted to become a nun could do so without a dowry needing to be paid.

It was a frugal life, but times in general were hard. Until the mid 1970's the hooded West Cork cloak was still occasionally seen being worn on the streets of Clonakilty and there were people in Clonakilty still suffering from want. The nuns delivered many helpful baskets of food to needy households on Sunday after lunch. We nuns still wore our long black serge habits even when I was with students who played in the volleyball championships in Bristol in 1980. The habit finally changed to short dresses and veils in the 1990's and the wearing of them is now optional.

Once I had taken my orders I trained as a teacher of Home Economics. The choice of training was decided by the needs of the time and for the good of the school. Our teaching salaries were paid into the religious community fund for the upkeep of all the community. At the time, a portion of the salary of any sister teaching science was put into a special fund that was used in the school to encourage the teaching of science subjects to girls and to provide facilities that were not grant aided.

As a teacher, over time I have noticed changes in the expectations of the parents of our pupils. Earlier in my career the majority of parents turned up to the school parent/teacher evenings and were deeply interested in who their child was becoming. In later years fewer parents came but the focus became more sharply upon the results their child was achieving. The teaching of skills rather than knowledge has become downgraded and is no longer valued in the urge to have every child going on to college, whether they are suited to it or not.

So, Sacred Heart Secondary School formed a bigger part of my life than I ever dreamed it would when I first unpacked my belongings there. It was the dominant part of it for almost 40 years. It formed me into who I am. The interaction with students, teachers, parents and the wider community was enriching. It is such a vibrant and caring community to work in and with: community being the important word. There is a sense of pride and care that is tangible.

****

Mary O'Donovan (Taylor) O'Regan

My first book "Women Speak, Life for Clonakilty Women in the 1900's", featured this beautiful young woman on the front cover. I noticed her portrait in Kevin O'Regan's shoe-shop window as part of a historical display for one of the many weekend festivals of the Clonakilty summer.

Unfortunately, I never met Mary as our paths never crossed in Clonakilty, but her family told me that the photograph was taken in Boston when Mary was 18 years old. Mary, like so many young Irish women, had endured a long sea voyage to join her sister in Boston, but after six months there was recalled home to . She lived at 36 McCurtain Hill, married Ted O'Regan and they raised three children, James (Jimmy), Aiden and Joan. She passed away in 2005 in her mid-nineties.

The stories from the first book are all included in this volume. AW

A Registered Nurse

My early life was spent in the town of my birth, Skibbereen, and I have vivid memories of my time there. We lived in Glencurragh, in a group of five or six houses adjacent to the GAA pitch. I was the eldest of three children and a terrible tomboy. I played with the neighbouring boys, some of whom grew up to be county footballers. Mrs Daly, who we called Nana, lived next door and was very kind to us. She had a sweet jar that was never empty and was forever giving us mints. We also had a neighbourhood Bonfire night at Halloween, or to celebrate when someone won something at football. So, we had great fun living in such a friendly place.

In the mid 1970's my father's Army job required him to work in Bandon and so the family moved to Clonakilty when I was about six or seven years old. We came to Clonakilty because my mother did not know anyone in Bandon. Clonakilty suited her better, as my father's sister lived there. At seven years of age I moved school to St Josephs National School for girls in Clonakilty. It was not a difficult time for me because as a new girl, everyone wanted to be my friend. Also, I was lucky to have a cousin who helped me assimilate into her gang initially. After I had learnt the ropes, I made my own group of friends. At St Joseph's when I was there, about half the teaching staff were religious sisters and half were lay teachers.

From St Josephs I went on to attend the neighbouring Sacred Heart Secondary School where the majority were lay teachers. I loved school especially the many extracurricular activities and in particular the drama classes held on site on Fridays. Eileen Nolan, the director of Montfort's School of Performing Arts in Cork, ran them. Drama had a huge influence on me and I was involved in most of the school shows. I nearly always had one of the male leading parts, due to my voice being stronger in the lower register and my above average height. Eileen was a super confident person and her confidence rubbed off on me. Growing up as the eldest and having lots of opportunities to play as an equal with boys also helped.

One of the most important influences of my school life was the core group of friends I built up then, who are still my friends today. Some of them moved away from Clonakilty for work or training, but most came back again. At school, we were encouraged to look after our friends and this has resulted in the wonderful outcome of long enduring friendships. At secondary school, I had decided that I would like to train as a nurse, just like my mother. She and my uncle both qualified in English hospitals and worked there prior to marrying and returning to Ireland. Although my mother did not register to practice in Ireland, she was always the one in the family and neighbourhood who patched people up, or advised them on medical matters. Doctors were not the first port of call then, like they are today. People had the mind-set that unless you were very ill you didn't bother the doctor. They were also very expensive.

My sister and I had jobs to do at home each Saturday morning before we were allowed outside. All the beds had to be made, the bathroom cleaned, hoovering[39] had to be done, including dusting the stairs and there was silver to be cleaned. We usually shared out the cleaning by choosing either upstairs or downstairs to complete. We were paid pocket money but I can't remember what we spent it on, as we were not into comics like some of our peers. From the age of 16 I also worked in the hospitality industry in the summer holidays, six days a week through to school

---

[39] Vacuum cleaning, called so after a popular brand of vacuum cleaner, the Hoover.

starting in September. We used to hitch a ride to and from the old Inchydoney Hotel and got paid 40 Irish pounds per week for waitressing. Lots of people hitched rides in those days and it was relatively safe, as fewer people owned private cars. I think I gave about 50% of what I earned to my parents and probably spent the rest on things like clothes and cigarettes. We used to take the bus up to Cork to shop for clothes at Penneys. There used to be a cinema in Clonakilty, on the corner opposite the An Sugan, that reopened in the mid 1970's and I do remember going there occasionally. Then it closed again about the mid 1980's due to safety reasons, I think. We always had a TV at home, a black and white one at first, then I recall getting colour and in 1978 RTÉ 2 coming on line, and finally getting the remote control. We also played a lot of games and cards as a family like: 25:45, Knock, Pontoon or Blackjack. My friends and I mostly met our boyfriends through our friends, clubs, sports or other groups.

I sat and passed my Leaving Certificate but due to the depressed economic times had no luck in gaining a place in an Irish teaching hospital. So, I completed a secretarial course to fill in time until I was accepted for a course at St Georges in London. I had already met my husband-to-be at this stage and he accompanied me on the boat trip to London, to help me settle, in June 1988.

Nursing training in England at that time was an apprenticeship type course where you worked on the wards as full-time staff, as well as having periods of classroom study during the course of three years of training. Our accommodation was in Tooting, in special nursing and medical staff flats. I shared one with three Irish girls. My flat mates in Tooting were allocated by the nursing school and I knew one of them, as she was a boarder in the secondary school I attended as a day pupil. We became great friends and are still in contact today.

We started with a three-month long block of lessons on general medical ward nursing, followed by practical experience and basic patient care in the wards. We then progressed to surgical nursing classes followed by surgical nursing patient care, and so on. At the end of our first year we had to sit and pass the Preliminary Exams to progress further. It was after passing the exams that I realised that I did not feel settled in England. The girls in London tried to dissuade me from leaving as I was doing so well, but I returned to Clonakilty. I had secured a place to begin my training again in September 1990 at the Cork Regional Hospital, but then I opted to get married. It was not deemed possible then to be a student nurse and a married woman, so I began a job at Harrington's pharmacy instead.

Getting married was a rather complicated thing to organise given that my husband was born into the Church of Ireland and I was Roman Catholic[40]. We visited both churches together and I felt warmly welcomed into the Church of Ireland congregation and there was no question about my taking communion there.

Whereas, I felt that my husband had a very different experience from the hierarchy of the Catholic Church, where he was treated as an outsider and every obstacle was thrown in his path. We had to be interviewed by the Parish Priest who wanted us to sign a document saying we would bring up our children in the Catholic faith, which neither of us was willing to do. Because we were "a mixed" couple we could not attend the local compulsory pre-marriage course but had to travel to Dublin for a special "mixed

---

[40] The chief difference is that the Catholic Church is under the jurisdiction of the Pope and the Church of Ireland is not. This results in certain important differences of belief and practice.

However, it should be noted that "the beliefs and practices held in common, greatly outweigh those that separate the two Churches." To learn more see www. http://ireland.anglican.org/information/6.

marriage" course. Despite two or three meetings with the Parish Priest he ultimately dismissed us and handed us over to a young curate who was much more understanding.

According to the Catholic Parish Priest a Church of Ireland Minister was not allowed to participate in the wedding nor take communion in the Catholic Church. So, on the morning of our wedding my husband and I went separately to take communion in our own churches. The young curate performed the marriage ceremony in the beautiful Catholic Church in Clonakilty, allowing the Church of Ireland priest to play a small role. Later, when the children arrived we decided to christen them in the Church of Ireland. In addition, our children made their First Holy Communion in the Roman Catholic Church and were also confirmed in the Church of Ireland. This allows them to have a free choice in the future as to which church they prefer.

At 21 years old, I was one of the first in my group of friends to marry. Most girls married in their mid-twenties then and we all started our families within a couple of years. I had the usual big Irish wedding with friends and family included and wore the traditional white dress. Our honeymoon was a two-week holiday visiting Cyprus, Egypt, Jerusalem and Lebanon. ,

I continued to work at Harrington's as our family grew. Being diabetic, I was not that well during the third pregnancy and gave up work, as I was also busy at home. My thoughts began to turn towards nursing again. So, it wasn't until 1997 that I finally went back to finish my training, when I was the mother of three young children between 9 months, and five years of age.

This time I had to begin again at the start, as the training system in Ireland had changed to a full time three-year course in University College Cork. We had lectures both in college and some in the hospital connected to the university (now known as Cork University Hospital). Placement weeks of block study in the classroom alternated with periods of practical experience, supposedly as a helper and observer on the wards. But in reality, we were scheduled as an essential part of the workforce.

Initially we went to college Monday to Friday for three months, but when working shifts in the hospital we had to do our quota of night duty. Usually it was six nights on, followed by four days off then back to day shifts again. It worked out at four to five weeks of nights for every two or three months working on the wards.

As a newly qualified staff nurse pending registration I was allocated to the operating theatres when my training was completed. It was not my choice to do so, but I came to really enjoy theatre work. I worked one weekend every six weeks on call. This meant that I would say goodbye to the three children on Friday morning and leave to drive to Cork to work in theatre from 7.45am to 7pm. As I could be called in to the hospital at any time on the Saturday and/or Sunday I stayed with my sister in Cork. Then I would work another 7.45am to 7pm day on Monday, arriving home after all the children were in bed. Tuesday, I worked a short day. This gave me a 40-45 hour working week. I was very lucky to have a husband who worked for himself farming and two sets of supportive grandparents to help with children, and who were really the only reason I could work the hours I did.

I qualified as a Registered Nurse in 2000. Working in Cork was not easy and I was delighted to be offered the opportunity to cover surgery nurse duties for a General Practitioner girlfriend in Clonakilty, when we both had young families. I am working three and a half days a week as a surgery nurse now, which I really love and fits in well with my family life too.

Clonakilty Traveller Women

Irish Travellers are a distinct ethnic and cultural group that have been a part of the Irish countryside for centuries[41], but their precise history is obscure due to the lack of written records. Prejudice and discrimination have added to their separateness. Traditionally nomadic, they roamed the land offering manual labour or handcrafted items in exchange for food and a place to camp. Some Irish Traveller groups have emigrated to the USA and others to the United Kingdom, where they maintain their separate identity. Around 25,000 Travellers are estimated to live in Ireland currently.

There are significant issues for Irish Travellers with poor housing, education and health leading to a lower life expectancy. Since the 1960's the Irish Government has made efforts to solve , which was often without basic sanitary amenities and electricity. In order to assimilate people into the community, public housing has been made available along with funds for education and welfare.

In the late 1990's there were still several encampments on public roads near Clonakilty where families were living in small clusters of modern style caravans and trailer homes, with laundry pegged out on the fences to dry. These have mostly disappeared from the area at the time of writing.

I visited The West Cork Travellers' Centre in Clonakilty in October 2014 to explain to the small group of women there that I would like to include some of their experiences in this book.

The women were sitting around a table in the bright and attractive room with delicious smells of the dinner they

---

[41] For more information about Irish Travellers see the website: www.itmtrav.ie/

were cooking in the air. Together they explained to me how the West Cork Traveller's Centre had helped them over the years. Some of the women were keen for me to write up their individual stories, as they had done so before, but had subsequently lost them during floods. I did this for those interested and sent them copies to keep. However, here I have noted some of the typical experiences they recalled.

Notes from a group discussion

Caroline Deere, who has sadly passed away, was the first co-ordinator of the Women's Group and in 1981 she started us off with hand sewing projects like patchwork cushion covers and quilts. We also made tablecloths and tissue box covers and learned knitting. At the time, we were all living in barrel top horse-drawn homes and manufactured caravans as the council were building houses for us. The barrel tops were great in summer but cold in winter. Many of us were parked at Shannonvale and on Moses Rd. One day a week we were collected from our homes at 8pm and driven into Clonakilty where we met in a room in the old school. We finished at 10.30pm and were then driven home again. Most of us came in family groups. We were also encouraged to take part in FÁS[42] schemes where we learned subjects like: reading and writing, housekeeping, gardening, family problem solving, health and parenting skills. Around 1997 Skibbereen and Bandon Traveller women also joined our group. There was a separate group in Bantry.

---

[42] FÁS - Irish National Training and Employment Authority

One traveller woman's experience

In the summer time, we would go out in the fields on jobs like picking potatoes and carrots and putting them into timber crates. We got paid in money for the work as well as milk, brown cake[43], and grazing for our animals. At Christmas time, we would make a 'Call back' to the farms where we had worked. We would take gifts of paper flowers and often would collect bits and pieces of furniture or other things that the farm family had put by for us and maybe a few quid[44]. We also at other times of year called back to exchange things like flowers, clothes pegs, safety pins, combs or camphor balls, for butter, sugar and eggs for our children.

We can't park on the sides of the road anymore and are fined if we do. The custom of burning the caravan after the death of a resident is done to set the spirit of the departed one free. Apart from keeping a few mementoes for the grandchildren or horseshoes for luck, it also bought peace to the families, as there was no fighting over the loved one's possessions.

Another traveller woman's experience

In the 1960's and the early 1970's in summer we went in a trap and pony that was driven alongside the barrel top wagon. Some of us kids liked it, but others did not. I loved being out in the fresh air and the freedom of it. It was fun getting away from the house and meeting loads of people on the roads. Sometimes tourists wanted to take our pictures and people often gave us things.

---

[43] Another name for brown soda bread
[44] Pounds or Euros.

Decorated Barrel Top Wagon at Blarney Castle

My father always built up his own camp. He used to tie pairs of long thin ash tree branches into half hoop shapes and dig the ends into the ground to form a tunnel. Then he tied a cover over the hoops to make up a tent. Our beds were made out of bales of straw and old clothes would be used to make a pillow. All the cooking was done over an open fire using old pots and a kettle to hold the food. In exchange for labour, people in the farmhouses gave meat, eggs and milk. We got water from streams and washed our clothes and ourselves in them too. If there was no stream we sometimes would carry water from a hose-pipe to our galvanised iron tub. The wet things would be draped over bushes to dry.

Eventually due to ill health my parents had to give up travelling. They were given a Council house to rent. It broke their hearts to do so because they couldn't keep what they wanted. Because they had only a small garden and were not allowed to have horses or other animals, they felt they had no freedom at all. My father had loved to travel and live on the roadside and they always cleaned up after themselves and never left a mess behind."

****

Margaret O'Driscoll

Travellers who live permanently in houses are called Settled Travellers. Margaret is a Settled Traveller who talked about her life.

My parents were Settled Travellers[45] living in a Council house in Skibbereen. I was born in the mid 1950's and at 14 years of age I was living with them and going to school by day. At 4pm seven days a week I went to my job at the West Cork Hotel where I worked until 2am. I left school when I was in sixth class and took a job cleaning vegetables in a local vegetable factory as well as continuing waitressing and wash-up work at the West Cork Hotel.

I was 17 when I met my husband, a Clonakilty Settled Traveller, at the Rosscarbery Horse Fair. I wore a white dress and veil when Father Walsh in Skibbereen married us later that year. The wedding reception was held at home. There was no hotel that would host a Traveller wedding then, even if someone had the money for it. We couldn't afford it anyway. I kept on working after we were married but I moved to a candle factory during the day and kept on at the hotel at night until I had my first baby. We lived alongside my mother's house in a caravan. My husband made his living by trading in horses and firewood.

My first child, Margaret, was born in Skibbereen Hospital when I was 18 years old. When she was four months old, as on every evening, she was bathed, fed, wrapped up warmly and put to bed. But when it was time

---

[45] On March 1, 2017, the Taoiseach (Prime Minister) Enda Kenny formally recognised travellers as a distinct group within the State. Mr Kenny said: "Our Traveller community is an integral part of our society for over a millennium, with their own distinct identity - a people within our people." The Taoiseach also said: "We recognise the inequalities and discrimination that the Traveller community faces."

for her 6am bottle we found her stone dead. I still haven't got over the tragedy of it. As was the custom in Traveller families, we then burned the caravan to free the spirit of the little one. My parents left their house too as there were too many sad memories of their dead baby granddaughter and we all came to live in Clonakilty. We were parked out by The Miles, with my parents in their caravan alongside ours. I was expecting my second baby by then and my husband and I were given a bungalow by the Council on Moses Road. It was in very bad condition and very cold and damp. The Council put us into anything just to get us off the road.

I had 12 pregnancies in all, as there was no way you could avoid pregnancy then. Most of my babies were born at St Finbarr's in Cork and everyone was always very good to me there. Big families were common and people had to beg from door to door to get things for their babies. Two of my pregnancies were miscarriages, and three were cot deaths. One of the little girls was born partly paralysed, possibly because she was delivered with forceps. She spent most of her short three years in hospital in Cork. We got a call one day when we were on our way to visit to say she had died unexpectedly. I bottle fed all my children because I always worked, that way my husband and others could help out by feeding the baby.

Because the Moses Road house was no longer suitable for us we were given a new four-bedroom house in Tawnies where we lived together. It was a lovely home, but my husband wanted to go and live in the countryside so we moved to a bungalow at Springmount. All my girls went to school in Clonakilty. Mary stayed on to get her Leaving Certificate and she has Child Care Certificates too now. Kathleen works in O'Donovan's hotel and lives in Casement Park, and another girl is married with three kids and working in a nursing home in Cork. Sylvia, the

145

youngest girl who has a certificate for hairdressing, lives with me and has been waiting for a house for nine years. Her little girl is two years old. There are four of us in this tiny two-bedroom house. My son living in Ballincollig is married, and another son in Leap has his own restaurant there. I would not let any of my four daughters go with Travellers, as it is a very hard life. All my seven surviving children have settled people as partners.

While my girls were still at school I worked for Fionnuala in her Italian Restaurant on Ashe Street for five years. My job was setting up the kitchen each day and doing the wash-up. Fionnuala was like a second mother to me and was very generous. She gave me left over food and things she no longer needed plus a gift at Christmas. She also paid my daughter Sylvia to help out there too. I have also worked in the kitchens at Golden Meadows and Mt Carmel hospitals. I am not working now as I am doing a FAS course in kitchen skills, which finishes early in 2015.

The people of Clonakilty that know me have been wonderful to me, dropping off bags of clothes, curtains, toys and bedding at the door. I am always so grateful and happy to get help that way. If I can't use things myself I hand them on to others who can use them. The nuns from Rosscarbery have also been very good bringing stuff for the house and at Christmas. The local St Vincent De Paul people do not seem much interested in helping Travellers. The only thing I ever get from them is a bag of coal at Christmas. My husband and I split up and I now have my own place in Clonakilty. One daughter lives with her father at Springmount because she and her baby of six months have been waiting for a Council house for 11 years. Her brother lives there too. All the Traveller families that I know are Catholic and most follow the Catholic teachings. While marriage is preferred, often young people live with each other for three or four years before they marry to see if it will work out.

I think that the Council are very prejudiced against Travellers and don't treat them the same as other young people on their list. They don't treat everyone looking for a council house equally and fairly. I also don't agree with the way that the Gards turn up whenever there is a Traveller funeral. It seems disrespectful and is discrimination. At one stage my daughters and I used to get followed around by a security guard in Dunnes Stores whenever we visited. I made a complaint to the manager and it stopped then. Another time I was very embarrassed there, when I overheard a woman customer saying to her friend, "Look at that, the knackers [46] are having black babies now", because Sylvia's daughter's father is dark skinned. It was racial discrimination against the baby and ourselves. I was so angry I told her so and gave her a good telling off.

Apart from these things I am happy with my life now but I still grieve for the three little ones. They are buried inside the Skibbereen cemetery and I go there to put fresh flowers on their graves every week. If I had to live my life over again I probably wouldn't do anything differently, except perhaps to try and get a job at the Cope Foundation. I think I would have really enjoyed working with people with disabilities.

****

---

[46] Unpleasant derogatory term.

Joan O'Donoghue

I was fourteen when my sister and I came to live in Clonakilty as Sacred Heart Secondary School (SHSS) pupils and residents of the Mary Immaculate Boarding School on Mt Carmel. There were 58 other pupils in the boarding facility, which had only been in existence for two years.

We lived on the top floor of the school and in the 1960's students who were sisters were housed in a separate dormitory. Very small cubicles were screened from each other by an arrangement of curtains and partial walls. Each contained a double bed that we shared and lockers for our indoor clothing. All the boarders were locked in at night, with a nun sleeping on the same floor. In retrospect, it seemed like a big fire risk and I never remember taking part in a fire drill.

Our days began when a nun ringing a bell arrived at our cubicle with a cup of holy water that was thrust through the curtains. As each of us took the water to bless ourselves, she would know we were out of bed. We each fetched cold water from the only tap on the floor in our basins and washed before daily Mass at 8am. After Mass, we ate a good breakfast in the refectory. I remember delicious brown bread, butter, boiled eggs, and cornflakes. Some of the girls did not like the boiled eggs and would stuff them into their gym tunics to pass on to the day pupils to dispose of. We could each bring our own supply of jam. I cherished a jar of lemon curd as an absolute luxury if I was ever lucky enough to have one. Once breakfast was over we had jobs to do, clearing tables, washing up, drying and polishing until the school day began at 9am.

Tuition fees were due for all secondary pupils until 1966 when free secondary education was introduced in Ireland. Until then the Fees at SHSS began at £6 per pupil, increasing annually to £12. Science was not part of the curriculum for girls until 1964.

At midday, we had dinner and then tea when classes finished at 3.30pm. Homework was supervised before and after supper at 7.30pm. Before bed at 10pm there was also a recreation period where we would do drill and pastimes such as Irish dancing. The school library also provided some diversion. Of course, we did not always lie down like good girls and sleep after lights out. We threw back the curtains and had loads of fun talking and laughing quietly.

Baths were taken weekly on a rota basis. Our modesty was preserved there by privacy, but how mortifyingly embarrassed we were if we got sick and Dr Collins was called, because we had to pull up our vests for him to examine our chests. However, if we were sick in bed we were always given the treat of a hot orange cordial drink and an apple at 4pm.

On Saturday mornings, we had classes as well, and later our chores to do, cleaning out our lockers, polishing shoes. We were never allowed outside the school unless supervised and would all be taken in to town to confession at the church there. On Sunday mornings, we dressed in our Sunday uniform to go to church, and as we hardly saw a young male from one week's end to the next, we all had crushes (unrequited of course) on the altar boys. In the afternoons, we would go in procession on supervised walks, sometimes in the countryside to Inchydoney Island, or Ballinascarthy.

Some of the girls were lucky enough to have visits from family and friends, but we did not. I was four years in the Boarding School where we stayed with the exception of school holidays. After we gained our Leaving Certificate results we were all called to the Principal's office and asked if we had any leanings toward religious life. I did not and left to train as a nurse. I would have preferred to go to university and work with numbers, but nursing was one of the few ways of gaining a qualification with accommodation supplied, while in paid employment.

Overall, I felt very fortunate during my school days. The nuns were good to me. Despite the narrow confines of life at boarding school, I was well looked after, gained a good education and made lifelong friends.

****

Requirements for Boarders

List from Sacred Heart Secondary School Jubilee Year Book 1991:

1 navy coat & beret

1 dark bottle-green gym, tunic

1 dark fir-green round neck jumper without collar

1 dark fir-green cardigan

2 white blouses with long sleeves and shirt collar

3 coat hangers and 1 skirt hanger

1 pair light indoor shoes – brown

1 dressing gown and 1 pair of bedroom slippers

2 nightdresses or pyjamas

2 sets usual underclothing

1 green coat overall long sleeves

2 pairs blankets and 1 rug, 2 pairs sheets, 2 bolster cases

3 toilet towels, usual toilet requisites, sufficient stockings

2 knives, 2 forks, 3 spoons tea, soup, dessert) marked with initials

Tennis racket and shoes

Sunday uniform – skirt, blouse, blazer, scarf and beret

All these items must be clearly marked with the boarder's full name

Birth certificate, Boarding fee: £55.00 per year (laundry included) £100 for two sisters.

Payable in September and February.

Drill: 15/- per year, Music: 25/- per term extra.

****

Una

I was born in 1948 into a farming family of five girls and one boy. I was the third child and we all attended the local two teacher Primary school. It was a mile from the house and we walked every day providing that it wasn't raining too heavy. Our parents worked very hard in difficult times. As each child was born, a post office book was opened and the Childrens' Allowance, and any other spare money, was saved for our education. We were told on many occasions that our education was going to be our dowry! Our farm was located fifteen miles from the nearest Secondary School so when it came to education we were all sent to Boarding Schools.

My two older sisters and I attended the Presentation Convent School in Crosshaven, where all subjects were taught through the medium of Irish. In preparation for this I was sent, at age eleven, to Coláiste na Rinne near Dungarvan, Co. Waterford. By Christmas of that year I was a fluent Irish speaker and when I came home for the holiday, I amused the family by forgetting that English was the spoken word in our house. Having spent five years in Crosshaven I was lucky enough to get a 'call to training' which meant that I was offered a place in a Teacher Training College in Limerick – that is if my singing voice and sewing ability were to a certain standard! I reckon I just got dragged through each of those. Two years of very intensive work from 8.00am to 8.00pm prepared us as teachers and in 1969 I was fully trained and ready for work.

Imagine the freedom for me, having spent eight years in schools, where we were institutionalised to a degree. I shared a flat in the city with my two older sisters, Mary a nurse and Anne in Insurance. My first work was in Maria Assumpta School in Ballyphehane, Cork. My father had two aunts in the Presentation Order. They looked after their own in those days and I just got a phone call to say I had a job in one of their schools! I taught Second Class and loved the experience. I remember the Principal taking me under her wing and showing me how it was done in the real world. This was the best guidance anyone could get and I benefitted greatly by her hands-on approach.

In 1971, I married Richard, a dairy farmer and moved to live in Timoleague. My next job was teaching junior classes in a two-teacher school close to Dunmanway town. I was well experienced in two teacher schools having attended one myself but it was a huge change from teaching in a twenty-teacher school in the city. I missed the companionship of all the young teachers in my last school. The children however were wonderful, and again farming was a way of life that they soaked up. I remember the boys would rush to the windows when a tractor would pass to see who it was and what they were doing. I taught sewing to senior girls and to senior boys and girls. This was a challenge I enjoyed and we even made some Christmas cakes, which we decorated. It took me some time when I came to West Cork to get used to people speaking in directions, such as west to Clonakilty, or south to the Co-Op. However, I decided that this was a problem I had to deal with head on, as one day in school when I was teaching writing to Senior Infants, I experienced an unusual request. I wrote a sentence on the blackboard for the class to copy and then attended First & Second Class. Very quickly one little boy tugged at my sleeve and very politely asked me in a broad West Cork accent if he would go east or west the page! Now I travel as competently as anyone in all directions.

As I was well used to farming growing up, I now quite happily milked cows, fed calves, drove the tractor and worked on anything that was going on outside on the farm.

If truth were told, I preferred to work outside than inside. I always found housekeeping very repetitive and uninteresting. Our first baby, Jean, was born in 1973, a little girl. Having a new baby changed our lives completely. She was the first grandchild in both our families so we had no experience whatever in dealing with this new little person. The night we brought her home we didn't sleep a wink waiting for her to wake up! The birth itself was not too difficult. I was two weeks overdue so was put on drip around 9.00am and she was born at 12 noon. What I wasn't prepared for was the emotions that came to the surface and I think I cried a lot that first week. Back then giving birth had no comforts attached to it, with stirrups etc. but luckily, I knew the nurse who delivered my baby and we later became friends. Even though I had a private doctor he was late attending to the birth and we certainly weren't going to delay so that he could be there! I think that I was very ill prepared and rather naive as regards birth and motherhood. Luckily one of my sisters who is a trained midwife came home with me and baby and that was a great help.

That year I moved to Clonakilty Convent G.N.S. to teach as a Remedial Teacher visiting two schools. I trained for this by going to Cork to classes each Saturday and by visiting existing Remedial Teachers in other schools. I spent six years in this position, which I found rewarding especially when children improved and moved back to class.

Following a miscarriage in 1975, I noticed sores on the tips of my fingers and attended my GP, who sent me to a consultant. After tests I was diagnosed with an auto-immune disease called Scleroderma. I was familiar with this as I had an uncle who had died of it at age 52. This was a big upset and from then I lived my life with an attitude that it was going to be a short one. My husband had been advised that 5 years is what I had, but he told no one which I really appreciate some 40 years later. I was lucky too that my GP took it all in his stride and treated me as if life was normal. I became very adept at caring for my fingers, wearing gloves and staying inside when the weather became really cold.

I became pregnant again and had another little girl, Susan, in 1977. This was a great joy for us as we weren't sure if we would have any more children. Another girl was wonderful too as I know how great it is to have sisters all through life. The birth of a baby boy, Richard, in 1980 created great excitement and his two sisters loved to hold him and play with him. November 1981, I was pregnant and looking forward to another baby in February, but my waters broke and I went into premature labour. A baby boy was born and he lived just one day. This was such a tragedy for all the family. A loss like this fills your whole mind and being and you live it out over and over again in your mind. It took me many months to accept the loss and move forward. There is no doubt that having a family already was a great help, as life moves on and they must be looked after.

I went back to school after Christmas. In 1979, I had left the role of Remedial and returned to teaching mainstream. I taught Senior Infants. Breed, the teacher who worked next door to me was a great support through all my problems and she suggested that it would be a good idea for me to attend a club and have an interest or hobby.

Breed and I visited the local Community College and decided on a Furniture Restoration Course! Over the next six months I stripped, polished and covered my six mahogany, spoon back dining room chairs. In April of that year a Flower Club opened in town and we both went along on the first night. Each person who joined could bring along a flower design or a pot plant for the competition, so I took a design and she took a pot plant! When I look back now, we were very ambitious having never even taken a class. We loved the night, which consisted of a Flower Arranging Demonstration and a critique on our work followed by a cup of tea and a chat. Thus, began a lifelong interest in the flower world. In September, I took a series of classes and this set me on the road.

The Flower Club in Clonakilty has become my second home. I cannot praise enough the members of the club. Their friendship, their generosity, and their support have meant so much to me over the years. An interest in flower arranging and gardening has brought us all together in one big family. We have worked, travelled and competed together for many years. We have made many friends in other clubs all over the country but at the end of the day there is no place or club like your own! I had no garden to begin with but within a short time my interest grew there too and I have spent many happy hours out in the garden, digging and weeding. Many of my plants have come from club members, and now I like to think that I can give back to others, who are beginning on their flower journey.

School life continued through the 80's. This was a difficult time as the country was going through a recession. Interest rates soared and we paid 21% on a loan we had taken out to buy more land. There were no foreign holidays in those days and we were lucky if we got a weekend in Kerry during the summer months. In 1989, I became pregnant and after an anxious nine months I had a perfect baby boy, John. After my last experience, this was a very special baby and I have often said that he had three mothers, as my girls were in their teens and a new baby in the house was a huge delight. He was delightfully spoiled.

The children went to school each day with me, first to the Primary Schools in the town and then to the Secondary

Schools. Now, the girls tell me that it wasn't easy to be in a school where their mother taught! At this stage I had left Senior Infants and moved from class to class up through that school as far as Third Class. Then I was asked to move up to Sixth Class, which in the beginning was a challenge but I eventually loved it. I had 40 girls in the first Sixth Class I taught and I often smile when I hear people complain about 30 in a class. Our Principal took a career break in 1996, so I became Principal in her place. This was a very strange experience as I had been trained to teach and then I found myself in an office, overseeing the running of the school and staff. After two years of this, I knew that I wanted to return to class teaching, as it was what I really loved to do.

At the same time, I knew that my health was deteriorating and I felt that maybe I could recover in a class that was so familiar to me. Unfortunately, this didn't happen and I had to take sick leave. My doctor suggested that I should retire and concentrate on building up my health. Sadly, I did just that in the year 2000. I found this really difficult as I loved my job and school. It took two years to find my energy again and I am thankful to all who helped me on that journey.

****

Dena & Catherine O'Donovan

Although my twin brother and I lived with our family in Cork, every weekend and school were spent in Clonakilty. There were seven children in my family, but we two spent more time than the others at the family hotel, O'Donovan's. My earliest memory is of my brother driving his Dinky toy cars around the green swirls of the carpet pattern in the Drawing Room there. In the mid 1960's, from about the ages of nine to eleven, my brother and I had jobs; sheet folding, bottle sorting and polishing glasses. There was a house laundry on site and as we got older I was also entrusted with ironing.

The large function room now known as 'The Venue' used to be known as the 'The Dancehall'. It was the big band era and there was much entertainment each Saturday night with entertainers like Dicky Rock and local bands playing. There was very little alcohol consumed at such functions then, mainly soft drinks like Deasy's Orange and Cidona. Men and women sat in chairs lining each side of the dancehall, men on one side, women on the other. The chairs had legs made of tubular metal and our job was to crawl forward along the tunnel made by the chair legs, where people might be seated, and retrieve the empty glasses. We did this by crawling out again backwards as soon as we had enough to carry in our two hands, and then repeated the process again and again.

The Hotel was then a "Commercial Hotel" designed to assist the many travelling sales and business people. There were ten guest bedrooms, and ten identically numbered desks with a lamp and papers for business use in "The Commercial Room". There were ten corresponding tables in the dining room. The bar tender looked after reception as well, and also sold BP petrol from a bowser out the

158

front. When the first TV arrived ten armchairs were arrayed around it, in what is now known as the Green Room. The bar was the place for men to drink while couples or ladies were served in the Hotel Lounge Bar at the back of the house. They paid a penny more for the privilege of taking a drink there rather than in the front bar.

One of the distinctive women associated with the hotel was 'Miss Katty' or 'Aunty Kat', pictured above. Catherine O'Donovan was born in 1882. Never marrying, she ran the hotel herself from 1918 and rode to the hunt with Castletownshend authors Somerville and Ross as well as Lord Carbery from Castlefreke. She wore trousers, was one of the first females in Ireland to abandon the sidesaddle when riding horseback, and smoked in public. Over time she also reared several children from the extended family under her roof in the hotel and had 22 godchildren some of whom are still living. Aunty Kat and my great-grandfather were two of a family of 18 children, many of whom emigrated to the US or Canada.

When Aunty Kat returned from one of her extensive travels to visit her siblings she brought back a child whom she claimed was her sister's. However, it was believed by many locally to be her own son. Later as an adult, he came from America to live with her for a time, but it will never be known for sure if the relationship was so, as he sadly died prematurely from pneumonia while travelling just nine days after his marriage. Damp hotel beds were blamed for his sad demise.

Before Aunty Kat died she sold the hotel at a nominal rate to her grandnephew, our father Thomas, to avoid disagreements over succession. He was the only family member in the locality that had shown an interest in the hotel. Looked after by our father, Aunty Kat lived on in one of the rooms at the hotel until her death in 1954. After she passed away we heard stories of her quiet kindness to some of the more hard-up local families through her distribution of food from the hotel back door.

I attended St Angela's, the Ursuline Convent school in Cork and after leaving went to Lee Commercial College for a year. Following that I studied architectural draughtsmanship and town planning at CIT, then worked in architectural offices for a decade. I spent three years of that, after my father died, in Sydney. My sister Ann had emigrated there as a teacher, taking up an assisted £10.00 passage. Meanwhile, brother Tom had studied hotel management and took over running the hotel. I returned to Clonakilty to assist him around 1987.

At that time socialising in pubs was very much a male thing and usually only one or two women would make up the throng in the bar. I remember feeling very daunted standing behind the semi-circular bar of the time and having people two or three rows deep all focusing on me. Having to speak up loud and call out "time" was nerve wracking until I lost my shyness after a few weeks. Then, it was considered somewhat unseemly for women to drink beer. How times have changed. Now the bar usually has more women than men, all socialising in groups, and it is nothing to be serving them pints.

O'Donovan's Hotel has now been run by the same family for over 200 years, one of the longest in Ireland and is the hub of the Clonakilty community.

Introduction to Margaret Feen

This original life story was beautifully hand written, mostly in the 1980's, on unlined foolscap paper by the late Margaret Feen. In 2012, she generously and spontaneously gave it to me, as an unpublished document, to use in my project. I subsequently talked with Margaret on a number of occasions and have added additional information and explanations gained, in italics, or footnotes.

Margaret was an exceptional woman, with a wonderful intellect and excellent recall. I love her writing style for its simple clarity of expression and celebration of all the best things in life: the beauty of nature, the satisfaction of hard work well done and the joy in simple pleasures. As a long-term computer user, I can only marvel at her immaculate pages of perfect prose. She was unwell and confined to her home for some years before passing away in her 94th year, but she retained her very sharp mind and excellent recall. I think her memories will bring much pleasure to you, whether you are a local person, someone with an interest in the locality of Clonakilty, or someone like me from a different world altogether.

I visited with her on a number of occasions in 2013 and she was happy to add to her story by answering many questions that I had about her own life and life in in general, despite being confined to bed. I record more of her observations below:

"The Great Famine continued on until the 1890's in the Ardfield district and there was lasting poverty. In my youth in the 1920's the poorer people lived in small cottages with thatched roofs, where commonly up to seven people might share a room and sleep top and tail[47] in one bed. Often the

---

[47] Laying alternately head, feet, head, feet: rather than four heads on the pillow and four sets of feet at the opposite end.

fuel used was dried cow manure, which left a pungent smell in the neighbourhood when burnt.

We were fortunate to have a small but sturdy farmhouse. There were three rooms upstairs and two rooms down. Each of the upstairs rooms was a bedroom and each contained a bed, one for my parents, one for my two sisters and me to share and one for my three brothers. Downstairs was the kitchen, the sitting room and the parlour. The parlour was the room kept for special occasions like The Stations, and visitors. There was no bathroom but we had a few outbuildings at the back of the house. The farm had 20 acres and on this land, we had seven milking cows, pigs (sows and bonhams), turkeys, hens for chickens and eggs, geese and ducks. We supplied the local shops with what we produced. We walked to Ardfield School, a very old school. It was cold and draughty with one classroom. We children brought firewood from home to school, for the fire in the Principal's office. When we arrived home at 4.00 pm we ate a hot meal of potatoes and turnips, cooked in a three-legged pot on the open hearth. Sometimes we had bacon and cabbage and we also often ate fish, as there were many fishermen around. Mother dried mackerel in the summer and rubbed it with salt to preserve it. She also made black puddings. Our homework from school was done in the light of a paraffin oil lamp and the purchased wax candles.

Emigration took away many of the young people. The photograph of my brother and me was taken in the nineteen twenties when I was about ten years old. My sister was visiting and she posed us outside our Dunnycove, Ardfield farmhouse. Later, back home in Boston, she and had a coloured photograph made.

Women's role in the 1920's, when I was growing up, was only a degree above slavery (and I presume it was a little better than in the preceding generation). Men were lords and masters and ruled over their women with a rod of iron. The main feature of the times was a lack of respect, which showed in the huge families the women had to produce and care for in the most primitive conditions. Ireland then was mostly a land of very small farms. Previously, after years of possession by a neighbouring country, settlers were brought in and given all the good land, leaving very stony, poor unproductive little lots for the natives.

Women, along with producing a baby a year, had to help the men to break up the land to put potatoes in. Potatoes were the staple food. Indeed, I am sure that many Irish children never tasted any other kind of food if the money wasn't there to buy flour. Mothers went without in order to put a bit of food in their children's mouths. After the dreadful Famine, which devastated the country, the population was halved. Political figures started to get active and after another long struggle the landlords began renting some of their estates. People got more independent and were able to grow crops to support themselves.

I remember my own mother, the former Kate Hurley, and how hard she worked to rear seven of us on a small farm. Her work was made harder because my father was an invalid as a result of injury to his spinal cord. She was out in the morning at six o'clock to bring in the seven cows and milked them before my brothers were old enough to help. Food had to be prepared and fed to calves and pigs, poultry seen to, and all this before she called us for school. The fire had to be cleaned of ashes and got going with the kettle for the breakfast hanging over it to boil. We had tea and brown bread for breakfast, brown bread and a bottle of milk in our school bags for lunch. She had to go to the field to dig potatoes for the dinner, cook the (seldom) bit of bacon and vegetables to feed us all on our return from school, prepare for the evening chores and see that the animals were bedded then come in and help prepare the tea. This would be a typical day's work for most women along with the tub of washing, the mending and the darning, and making clothes for the family. Along with all that there was the farm work where she had to help, setting the potatoes in the spring, saving the harvest, and feeding hungry men. Everything that happened inside and out, the men expected the women to help. There was so much truth in the old saying, "A woman's work is never done." Technology and progress changed the face of women's labour but we must always remember the huge debt we owe them.

Emigration too made a big difference. Where with great difficulty, the fare to America was gathered for the first of the family, after a few years she was able to send for the next one and so on. What those brave girls went through alone in a strange land and having to adapt to city life and a totally new culture, and often managing to send a few dollars home to relieve the misery.

My Own Place

Looking back over the years and the decades it seems that I've been around a very long time. Ardfield, my native parish lies to the south of Clonakilty, a parish of headlands washed by the Atlantic, and a coastline dotted with ruined castles built by the land-owning class. The district too had its quota of "Big Houses": Boss Croker of Tammany Hall fame, the Hungerfords, Beamishes, Galweys: dwindling relics of the old landlord system.

The early twenties were an era of intense class distinction. The gentry still owned a big share of the land even though this stranglehold was broken by the land agitation under Parnell[48] and Davitt[49] while the farmers and cottiers[50] fiercely held on to their precious and hardly won acres.

Home for me, Dunnycove, was a small farm of reasonably good land and a typical West Cork farmhouse with traditional roses round the door. My mother had 'green fingers' and she had a magnificent sweet smelling 'Constance Spry' type of rose trailing round the door. Even the most sophisticated modern breeders could never surpass the heady perfume of that beautiful rose.

---

[48] Charles Stewart Parnell 1846-1891
[49] Michael Davitt 1846-1906
[50] A labourer renting a small portion of land, at a rent fixed by competition.

I was the youngest of six children with two sisters who had emigrated to Boston and three brothers. Our family life was different from our neighbours owing to the fact that my father was an invalid for as long as I can remember – crippled from the waist as a result of an accident. In those far off days there were neither operations, drugs nor injections and I can remember vividly his intense suffering, but his innate good humour. His courage and faith kept him going and made him an inspiration to everybody round him.

My birth coincided with the birth period of our Free State and I grew up with the "Young Ireland". Being born in the early twenties meant growing up in an intensely active political scene, and in spite of the fact that we lived at the extreme end of the country there was a very keen awareness of what was happening nationally. In my own family, this interest was accentuated by the fact that my father was a near relation of O'Donovan Rossa[51] and Michael Collins was born a few miles away in the next parish. Our only contact with the outside world was the "Cork Examiner" and even though it only cost 2 old pence very few people could afford it daily. The "Southern Star", while keeping its "eye on Russia" supplied us with all the local news.

School Days

Strangely enough I can't remember my first day at school. Having no sister, I was taken care of by my neighbour's daughter, a kind sensitive girl, Mary Esther. The school was a two-roomed building, cold and draughty with a fire at only at one end. In the very cold weather we had turns warming our hands a few times a day. There were two teachers one of whom taught the infants, first and second

---

[51] Jeremiah O'Donovan Rossa 1831-1915

classes, the other teacher had the third, fourth, fifth, sixth and seventh, about 80 pupils altogether. School in the 1920's was so different from modern times. We learned everything off by heart – poetry, spelling, grammar, tables, history, geography and catechism. We learned to write by using headlines, and with the aid of charts we identified everyday objects and learned how to put sentences together. As we progressed to the higher classes we had reading and spelling sessions and tried to grasp the intricacies of grammar and punctuation. The school programme, in retrospect, was a comprehensive one and we had needlework twice a week and nature study. There was often a jar of frogs' spawn at the window, and we observed their progress and imbibed the rudiments of biology from plant life. It was a very crowded schedule and the teacher had to have five different programmes going, to cater for classes from third to seventh. Overcrowding was an unknown term and at that time no child left school before 14 years at the earliest.

There were no school meals in the days of my youth. We walked the miles on a breakfast of tea and brown home-made bread and brought two slices of bread and butter and a bottle of milk for lunch, which we ate out in the yard on fine days and in bad weather we dined in the classroom – the second room in the school which acted as cloak room and general utility.

The standard of hygiene was primitive. The only pretence of washing facilities was a wash stand and basin and a bucket of cold water brought from a nearby well each morning, but we were hale and healthy and didn't know the meaning of the word "germs" which no doubt abounded in our antiquated dry toilets.

Our teachers were very hard working and dedicated, working under extreme handicaps to instil knowledge into unreceptive young minds. Indeed, they acted as nursemaids as well as teachers and always saw that the less well-off never went without a lunch. Even though corporal punishment was part of school life the stick was seldom used, the threat of it acted satisfactorily. In those young carefree days, we did not always appreciate the lessons we learnt and the religious foundation established by our teachers and we owe them a big debt of gratitude for their unselfish efforts on our behalf.

Heart of the Home

The kitchen was the centre of activity in every farm home. It was usually the biggest room in the house with an open fireplace and a fire machine[52], the wheel of which had to be turned by hand to create a good draught. The settle provided seating accommodation, and the big table and chairs were white wood and were taken outside on Saturday and scrubbed with sand. No comfort as regards flooring – the floor was cement and my mother scrubbed that too on Saturday night. A big cupboard held all the foodstuffs and, on the top shelf, the clothes that were needed from day to day. But the pride and joy of every country-woman's heart was the dresser. It was indeed 'filled with shining delph[53] speckled and white and blue and brown. On our dresser, there was a collection of Blue and Brown Willow, from the big meal dishes down to the teacups, jugs of all sizes, lovely lustre and floral patterns and rows of coloured basins. An average dresser would have at least 100 pieces and it was a major job taking them down and washing them and putting them back shining. The parlour was little used except maybe at Christmas and Stations time.

---

[52] A type of bellows
[53] China or crockery. Quote from the poem 'An Old Woman of the Roads' by Padraic Colum.

In every farm, there was a dairy or cool room. Those were for creamery days: Sir Horace Plunkett's co-operative movement had not yet reached West Cork. The milk was kept in big earthenware pans, having been strained and left to set. Once a week (or twice in summer) the cream was skimmed off and butter made in the churn. It was then washed well and wrapped in white cloths that were made from washed and boiled flour bags that had been bleached on the grass until they were as white as snow. Once wrapped the butter was taken to be sold in the local shops. The bleached flour bags were also used as sheets and pillowcases and of course tea cloths. A very versatile article the big hundredweight flour bag and it was possible then to buy them so cheaply in flourmills.

Washing was another big chore and the age of synthetics and other easily washed clothing wasn't even a dream at that stage. All the underclothes were heavy, the men usually wore flannel and the working shirts were strong and hard to wash. The water had to be boiled in the big iron pot and the clothes soaped on the table and scrubbed on the washboard. Anything boilable was boiled in the pot. The Sunday shirts were white and the men wore starched collars and fronts. It was possible to buy these detached.

My mother ironed with a box iron. She put the heaters into the fire until they glowed red and then, with the poker took them out, put them into the iron, closed the little doors and ironed away on the kitchen. On the starched collars, she used a special small glossing iron and rubbed away until they shone. When some years later we got a range, it changed the atmosphere of the kitchen. The open fire and fire machine were transferred to the "back kitchen" and most of the work was done there.

There was bread baked every day: big bastible cakes of brown flour milled from our own wheat. The bastible was heated over the flames and the cover "reddened" on the coals. When the cake was put into the red hot bastible, the cover was put on again with the poker, and the red coals put on top. Timing was incidental – according to the heat of the fire. Some people who could not afford coal or turf collected the dried cow-pats. It burned quite well but you would get the smell a mile away!

I was always the best-dressed girl in school as my clothes were all hand-me-downs from a well-off cousin in Dunmanway. As I was the youngest child in the family my mother also had time to make things for me, either knitted or crocheted. I well remember the lovely collar, bonnet and gloves she made me from navy blue wool with a band of white fur around the face, neck and wrists. Being the youngest child was a privileged place to be. However, it was a disadvantage when it came to caring for babies and children, as I knew nothing of them until I had my own. Our farmhouse was a typical one of the times, with two rooms downstairs and three rooms upstairs. You entered the house via the kitchen, which had the stairs to the bedrooms on one side, and the kitchen led into the sitting room. The outhouses were to the side of the house.

Entertainment

Growing up in an era of great political activity we learned and sang mostly patriotic songs both at school and at home. Young people today would find it impossible to visualise life without radio, TV and other technology, but that precisely was the situation. My sister on a visit home from Boston brought a gramophone and what a novelty it was. It was played so often that the records were worn out in a short time. Our nearest neighbour's son was a radio officer on a ship and brought home a battery-operated radio. That was the eighth wonder of the world and we could not figure out the intricacies of it. The batteries had to be charged at regular intervals in a garage and we were able to hear (with luck) the news and the matches from Croke Park. There was always an overflow audience on such occasions. People in the country created their own amusement in those days and in our house, we had a ceilidh[54] every Sunday night. The kitchen table was put outside and my father played the melodeon[55] and twenty or more young and not so young people danced the sets, waltzes, military two steps, long and short schottise, Walls of Limerick and Bridge of Athlone. Most of the young people of the area learned to dance on our kitchen floor. Everything started early and ten o'clock was the deadline, as everybody had to be home by ten thirty.

Again, probably because my father was an invalid, we always had neighbours in at night "scoraiochting" and many a hair-raising ghost story was told around the big fire of wood. The old people excelled at storytelling and most of them believed in or had a healthy respect for the "little folk". I often sat frozen in my seat under the chimney listening to the tales of the witchery of the "Sprid a Camus" who intercepted any traveller who had occasion to be out before cock-crow, and "Crapa leasa" who allegedly roamed the graveyards with chains dangling. Later though we found out that the chains turned out to be the tying on Tim Jack's donkey's legs, which lived in the field adjacent to the graveyard.

All the happenings of the parish and beyond were discussed at that fireside. My father read anything interesting out of the paper, and when we only got the odd paper everything was of interest. When my mother went to town we got "Our Boys" or maybe "Ireland's Own". We were lucky in as far as reading was concerned in that a cousin in Kildare who was involved in horses sent my

---

[54] A social event with traditional, singing dancing and story telling.
[55] A small accordion

father a parcel of books regularly. By the time I reached ten years I had read more of Nat Gould's books than any punter in the Curragh and I was in on any elusive movement of the Scarlet Pimpernel. At Christmas, there was always "Girls Annual" in the parcel: what a lovely treat they were and I shared them with my best friends.

I never remember a pair of shop socks coming into our house in my young days. My mother knitted all the socks for my father and brothers. Indeed, I can truly say her hands were never idle. She made quilts with little baubles of white cotton thread, she covered old blankets with cotton cretonne, she made crochet shawls and bonnets. All that as well as mending and darning the heavy working clothes at the end of a heavy day's work in the indifferent light of the lamp on the wall.

Meitheal[56] Memories

Looking back to those far off days it was a miracle how people got through so much work with so few conveniences. Starting at about 6am in summer the cows had to be brought in and milked, the milk strained and put to set in the dairy, and the cows and pigs fed and we always had a few little ones which needed constant attention. Owing to my father's health problem my mother had much extra work and while my brothers were young she had to work on the land as well. There were potatoes to be put in as well as having to cut the scillauns[57], hay to be saved and the harvest was an exceptionally busy time. Hay saving, we loved. It was a pleasant task to turn the rows of newly mown sweet-smelling hay and make it up into small cocks, which were later made into big ones. The cocks

---

[56] A group, often of neighbours, gathered together to perform a task, with some social element added.

[57] Seed potatoes.

were brought into the haggard in an operation known as "slinging". It was done by encircling the cocks with a strong rope which was attached to the horse, and many the tumble we got off the cocks when we were let ride on them. But it was all glorious fun and the loveliest part of all was the tea in the hayfield. My mother brought out a sweet-tin [58] of strong hot tea and currant cake and no Cordon Bleu Cuisine could ever taste as good as that feast on a lovely June day. Maybe nostalgia makes everything seem rosy, but I am sure that it was a fact that in the 1920's and 1930's the seasons came in their proper times and from May to September there was very little rain and the long hot summers made the work of saving the harvest much easier. I can't help thinking how much today's children are missing out on. Silage harvesters have taken all the fun out of haymaking. No longer is the big thatched rick in the haggard [59]. Mechanisation has changed the whole leisurely farming scene to one of big noisy machines, smelly silage and impersonality. When the hay was safe in the haggard and the rick snugly thatched the corn was ripening and the biggest task of the year was upon us – the cutting and harvesting of the grain. The corn [60] was cut with a mowing machine drawn by two horses but I can remember seeing scythes being used and even hooks in very small areas. The children usually got the task of 'picking the sops' – gathering the stray straws after the sheaves were bound. The sheaves were then stooked, four in each side with heads meeting and with room to let the wind through to dry them well. The next stage of stacking needed a big effort and it was the children's job to draw the stooks together for hand stacks.

---

[58] A recycled tin from a sweet shop, with a lid and wire handle.

[59] The area close to the house where the hay shed and corn ricks were.

[60] Common name for wheat.

These, after a few days drying in the sun, were brought into the haggard to await the coming of the threshing engine.

Threshing was 'D' day and because it happened in September we had the added bonus of a holiday from school. I can remember the horse driven thresher where four horses were driven round a circular area. They rotated an axle like piece of machinery, which connected by belts, drove the drum – the machine that separated the grain from the straw. This was where the meitheal gathered. All the neighbouring farmers "cored", that is, helped one another. Each man had his own task – picking sheaves off the stacks, cutting binders, feeding the sheaves into the drum, picking the straw out on one side and collecting the grain into sacks on the other side, winnowing, which meant separating the grain from the chaff in a hand operated machine, and of course making the rick.

Rick making was a highly specialised craft and certain men in each area were in great demand for this important task. The layers of straw were laid and packed well and the top shaped in roof form and thatched to withstand the wind and rain. Straw proved good feeding for cattle along with the hay and it was very important to have it well protected. Sugans[61] were made to tie down the rick and weighted with heavy stones. It could be sliced like a loaf of bread in the late autumn and winter.

The hustle and bustle of threshing day had to "be seen, to be understood". In the 1930's the horse work outfit was replaced with the petrol engine and later, the progression to the big steam engine took place. The demise of the meitheal came with the combine harvester and a completely new scene emerged in Irish farming, leaving the excitement and activity of threshing time only a memory.

---

[61] Straw ropes

The harvest was a time of plenty for man and beast. All the farmers grew wheat, oats and barley. The wheat was carefully stored in the loft for flour for the household. There were oats for the horses and barley was sold either to the milling companies in the town, or in the case of malting barley, it was sold to the brewery in Bandon for the production of whiskey.

Threshing day was one of intense activity for us children. We helped our mother to prepare food for the 30 or more hungry men, a herculean task and we had to collect extra cutlery and crockery from the neighbours. There were huge pots of potatoes, bacon and cabbage cooked and several very large currant cakes baked the day before as well as the mountain of shop-bread. It was all back breaking work but so satisfying, and tired as everybody was, there was always "a night" singing and dancing and the older men drinking porter, the younger ones got lemonade. The neighbours who did not have land to grow corn collected big bags of chaff, which they used to make mattresses. These and feather ticks were in use everywhere and it was quite some time later that the hair and fibre mattresses came into vogue.

When the corn was sold, all the bills incurred in the production: seed, manure, threshing costs etc. were paid and clothes and shoes purchased for the winter. The harvest was a happy rewarding time when the results of hard physical labour were brought to fruition. The farmers were able to balance their budgets and face the winter secure in the knowledge that their families and livestock were provided for the winter in the barns and the haggards.

In my rather long lifetime, nothing has changed more drastically than the Irish farming scene. I am thinking particularly of the dairying area and of cows – their hugely increased numbers and the unbelievably progressive methods of their care and maintenance.

176

Away back in the 1920's when I was growing up, the cows were then, as now, the mainstay of every farming family and were treated with respect and almost devotion. Young progressive farmers would find it hard to envisage the old type stall where the cows lived in comfort during the long winter months bedded in a thick layer of straw. Very few farmers had more than 10 cows, intimately known by individual names – Rosie, Daisy, Strawberry etc., and each animal had an identity with the regular milker. Women were considered to be better and more patient milkers and when a cow was restive – maybe with a sore teat - she responded to the soothing voice of the cailin[62] singing or talking to her, like, "Yeossh Rosie, easy girl". Heifers invariably had to be spancelled[63] for their first milking and the milker was often in a vulnerable position when a kick could land herself and the bucket in the passageway.

This was all so long ago, before electricity and milking machines were even a dream. Sir Horace Plunkett eased a lot of the hard work when he brought the Co-operative movement and the creameries to every part of the country. The last chore in the winter nights was to light the storm lantern and "go out to see the cows and horses". The warmth and comfort of the stall with contented animals munching sweet smelling hay laced with sliced turnips was probably too conducive to TB germs, but what comfort they lived in compared to the modern open yards. But that I suppose is progress. It has wiped out so many of the old customs like burning the udder hair off the newly calved cows and blessing them with the blessed candle and holy water. Another era, other traditions: who is to say that it wasn't a better life for man and beasts.

---

[62] Young girl
[63] Hind legs tied with rope

Summer jobs

The summer job is no new phenomenon and the six weeks break from school meant that there were plenty of jobs lined up for us on the farm. The harvest time we loved, but there were other less pleasant tasks. Thinning turnips and mangolds was hot work on a July day and the knees and fingers suffered from contact with the rough, dry earth. One chore that had to be done regardless was drawing water. Many young people nowadays would find it hard to realize that water did not always come at the turn of a tap, but in the parish where I grew up, the long hot summers were synonymous with water shortage. Most people relied on wells three or four feet deep that invariably dried about the end of May. In every locality, there were the precious few that never dried – treasures almost on a par with gold mines. Farmers had to travel miles in those days to draw water for households and animals.

I remember we had what was known as "the truck" – a low flat structure on wheels and capable of holding a 30 gallon barrel plus a smaller one. It was drawn by Jess, the donkey, a very strong-willed female who, without difficulty could find her way to the well and back a mile away. Those of course were the days when the roads were traffic free and a motorcar was a rarity. The well, Tobar na bhFeochadain", was never known to dry in spite of the fact that there was a succession of customers from morning till night. The buckets of water had to be brought up six steps to the barrels. When full they were covered with clean sacks held down by a hoop and because Jess was a slow mover, little of it was lost in transit.

Going to the well was a way of life when piped water was an unknown quantity in country areas, before rural electrification brought a whole new dimension to the scene. When the breakthrough came (in the 1950's) many years and countless barrels of water later, it changed the whole aspect of rural living and made the hard, physical work of man, woman and beast an unhappy memory.

Parents in the 1920's believed that busy children seldom got into mischief and without a doubt the well-balanced lives we led, not having much in the way of luxuries or entertainment made us happy and contented and appreciative of the little extras as rewards, that came our way occasionally.

In the cold winter evenings cutting turnips for the cattle was a cold hard chore. The turnips had to be put in a machine and the handle turned to slice them, and transported into the stall and calves house in baths. But hardest of all the chores was "bruising" furze for the horses. The furze machine was much like the turnip machine with a sharp knife-like blade and a handle to turn. The finer furze was easy enough to handle – it was transferred from the heap with a wooden implement called a Gabhlog but when the blade hit a stump it was full stop and much effort to get going again. The horses, strangely enough loved it and Jess always got her ration. It was hard going to get all the chores done before dark – no Electricity Supply Board then.

Fish and Fowl

The farmers in the 1920's had a great affinity with the land. They worked on it all day and at night around the fire they discussed every aspect of it. But there were a great many people in the area that had very little as regards property and poverty was rampant. One advantage the coastal areas had was the fishing and in those days, it was big business; indeed it was the lifeline of a great many families in the parish. The fishermen shared six or eight oared boats and rowed out miles to the fishing grounds. They knew where the different species of fish were to be found – whiting, pollock, bream, mackerel and herring. In summer, they often stayed out there three or four days or until the boats could hold no more. Their food consisted of yellow meal stirabout – the meal was boiled until thick and it cut like bread. That with water was the fishermen's diet. The fish was sold locally, or taken to Clonakilty. I remember my mother curing great quantities of it for winter. A great number of the people never tasted meat, but farmers usually cured their own bacon and what a treat it was when the pig was killed and the delectable fresh pork and pork steak was so enjoyed. There was always some for the neighbours and the remainder was salted and put in a barrel. My mother filled the intestines after thoroughly washing them, with a mixture of oatmeal, onions, salt, pepper and blood and then boiled the black puddings in the big pot with hay in the bottom to prevent burning. They were so delicious and they were shared with the neighbours.

We seldom had lamb or beef; perhaps at Christmas, but when my mother went to town she always bought a big piece of boiling beef and with that she made dumplings and cooked them with the meat. It was food fit for a king and we did justice to it.

The farmers in those days were almost self-sufficient. Every farmer grew at least an acre of potatoes for their own use and for feed for pigs and fowl. They grew cabbage, turnips, onions and carrots, always enough for the year. Nobody would even think of buying vegetables. They had butter from the milk, and the wheat according to what was needed, was taken to the mill. There were lots of mills in every country area, some very old stone mills and they ground either coarse or fine according to taste.

Then there were the fowl. My mother kept about 100 hens, free range of course. Deep litter was unheard of then.

As well as the hens she had turkeys and geese and ducks. She, as was the custom, hatched the eggs under "clucking hens". Usually a sitting was 13 or 14 eggs according to the size of the hen. Chickens took three weeks to incubate, turkeys and geese about four. The chickens were reared and fattened: the cocks (with the exception of the odd one for the table) were sold and the pullets kept replacing the old hens whose laying life was ended. The turkeys and geese were sold for the Christmas market and were a welcome source of revenue at a lean time of year. Turkeys were delicate birds and with the hazards of sickness as well as foxes you could truly not count them until you had the money in your hand.

Fun and Games

Our busy schedule left very little time for actual games in my young days. Those of us academically inclined and able to lay our hands on a book had great opportunities in the summer months when one of the regular tasks was minding the turkeys and chickens from the hawk and grey crow. We made daisy chains and fitted foxglove flowers (fairy thimbles) on our fingers. In the spring, we looked for birds' nests and vied with each other as to who had the biggest number. They were only to be looked at, not touched. We were warned that the mother bird would forsake the little ones if we did. The hedges and ditches were full of nests and alive with birdsong with no modern machinery or cars or trucks on the road to disturb them. The corncrake was "on the air" morning noon and night and the young birds were often saved at hay cutting time and put in a safe ditch. See-saw was a favourite pastime. We put a heavy plank across a low ditch[64] and one sat on each end. We sang little songs like "See-Saw, Jack in the

---

[64] A stone or earthen wall, often vegetation covered.

181

Pool". We had swings when we could prevail upon an adult to tie a rope upon a strong branch. At school, we played "Ring a Rosie" and "Spy" and "Chickens come flock". On wet days, we danced in the classroom at lunchtime and at Halloween we had "Snap Apple". Playing "Shop" was always a favourite and our merchandise was limited to stones and bits of coloured glass and sand, which we used for tea and sugar. Those were the days when packaging and tins were unknown. We had sack races and played hoops and in our simplicity created a lot of pleasure and happy memories which will always be with us.

The Village Shop

The shop cum Post Office, cum general store was almost a social centre for the area. It carried a huge selection of goods; grocery and provisions, bacon, dried fish, cups, saucers, jugs, basins, saucepans even knitting wool (Mahony's Blarney Fingering) for men's socks and long winter stockings for the young folk. One could buy ladies lisle stockings and little necessities like elastic and needles and thread. In the store attached there was coal and different kinds of animal feed like meal and bran and pollard. The only pretence of luxuries were the two penny packets of biscuits and quarter and half–pound packets of cream crackers and maybe the odd currant loaf.

Wednesdays and Fridays were hyperactive days at the shop. Wednesday was egg and butter day. The farmers brought the week's supply of butter and eggs and Paddy, the general factotum, packed the eggs between layers of straw into wooden crates and brought them in to the town to the egg store. He wrapped the slabs of butter in white cloths and they too were sold in the butter market. His form of transport was a pony and cart and he sat on top of the crates. Those were pre-creamery days and a barter system was in operation. The farmers and cottiers exchanged their produce for necessities like groceries, flour, animal feed etc. and very little money changed hands.

Business boomed on Friday, pension day. The pension at that time was ten shillings weekly, maximum, but in the twenties and thirties it provided the week's groceries for an average family.

The village shop did not provide "special offers" in its services but it was friendly and personal, and when times were bad, which they invariably were, at that time credit was never refused. Each customer had a "pass book" in which an account was kept in elementary book-keeping. At Christmas, everybody got generous "Christmas boxes" and often during the year there would be the odd currant loaf or pot of jam slipped into the basket. One wonders if we were better off in our simplicity compared with the present system.

We spent the infrequent pennies we could come by in a little sweet shop near the school. Two sisters (Coughlan) carried on a little business, really from a large press in their living room. Miss Coughlan made cones of newspapers and on a good day you might be lucky enough to get ten sweets for a penny. Sometimes they had caramels "Colleen Kisses" and they were sheer heaven. There was no talk of calories in those far off days, just pure luxury unspoilt. Sometimes too they got drumsticks – a gorgeous chocolate covered hard sweet on a stick and at two for a penny they were the ultimate.

Travelling visitors

Every area produces its individual characters and West Cork was no exception to that rule. In my young days, our unexciting lives were enlivened by the visit of one or other of the regulars who called once or twice a year and some of who were given a bed on the settle for the night. One I remember always in my prayers was Sean O, a mild soft-spoken man who worked with a farming family on the far side of Clonakilty. He had a brother in America who wrote to him every Christmas and sent him £5.00. My father wrote on Sean's behalf to thank him – it was an annual task. I did well on the transaction getting a whole shilling from Sean and indeed many a bag of sweets as well. He always stayed the night and was gone in the morning at sunrise – one of God's gentlemen, scrupulously clean, honest and God fearing.

A much more forcible visitor was Sean Sile. His travelling periods were interspersed with short holidays in a neighbour's farm where he paid for his keep by cutting wood, clearing overgrown ditches and tidying generally round the yard. Sean had a quick sharp tongue and when the Parish Priest lectured him about a "rolling stone gathering no moss". "No father", he replied, "but it has the scenery". Jack (or Sean) was very partial to the locally brewed black drink with the creamy head and spent many a night in the "guest room" of the Garda Barracks after a heated altercation with the officers of the law.

In complete contrast was the "Soda Bread Man", a quiet unassuming Mayo man. He adored brown bread and only stayed long enough to take a few cups of tea and brown bread and butter with a piece of the cake in his bag for the next day.

Kitty C was a lady with a touch of elegance. She always wore skirts almost to the ground and produced a bag from under her shawl, which contained needles, spools of strong black and white sewing thread and bits of coloured hair ribbon. It was to us children almost a Pandora's box and we loved to see her coming.

The "foxy woman" was a tall well-built lady with a head of fiery red hair. She too carried a basket, with religious objects like small statues and pictures. She had, if my memory serves me rightly, sixteen children, and was always on "the scrounge" for a bit of tea and sugar, bread or anything wearable. She brought first hand news of relations of ours who lived at the other end of the country – her travels were extensive.

Then there was Johnny Polly. He was a survivor of the 1914-18 war and he told us of how he laid under a dead soldier and pretended to be dead when the enemy scouted around. Needless to say, he always had a rapt audience and we got all the gory details of his precarious journey back to camp. His greeting invariably was "Seldom I come", so we christened him this.

There were many other "Knights of the road", each one highly individualistic. They had certain stopping off houses where they knew they were welcome and sure of a meal. They were colourful characters that brought a touch of adventure on their visits and always appreciated the hospitality they received.

St James Day

St James was the Patron Saint of Ardfield and his feast day was celebrated on the third Sunday in July. There was a holy well named after him in the area to which people went to pray and make rounds but I am afraid it wasn't the religious aspect of the feast that appealed to us children. Rather it was that travelling shops from Clonakilty came to the village on that day and great crowds gathered to celebrate. The goodies were displayed on flat carts covered with white sheets with an overhead cover to keep off the sun. For months before we saved every penny diligently and hoped it would be supplemented by the contributions of relations. A half crown[65] was the very most we could

---

[65] Two shillings and sixpence (30 pennies) in one coin.

hope for and we had to budget carefully on the day to stretch it as far as possible. The sugar stick was the biggest draw. That came in the way of thick sticks of delight made from brown sugar and butter plus some secret ingredient known only to the woman who made it. It sold by the penny worth. There were packets of biscuits, big rosy apples, lemonade, a rare treat and partaken with big currant buns - Bath Buns as they were known. But the gooseberries were the greatest of all - big luscious mouthfuls of sheer delectableness. They were sold by the pint and the supply never lasted long. The young people danced on a cement platform to the music of a melodeon. There was often a game of football in the field across the road and a score of bowls, which was always popular. The whole scene was so happy and relaxed and we looked forward to St James's Day for weeks before and even now, a lifetime after, we cherish the memories it invoked.

The Feast of Feasts

If anticipation is the greatest pleasure in life, the weeks leading up to Christmas were sheer heaven. December (Mi Na Nollag) the very name filled our young lives with pleasure. The Christmas cards were bought and posted to America and the turkeys were brought in off the stubbles plump and ready for market. They represented the housewife's "pin money" and their price determined the extent of the luxuries that could be afforded for the feasting. There was always great excitement when they were being taken to market by horse and cart in covered cribs, and many a Hail Mary went to them for a good price - at that time about sixpence per pound.

Christmas was the occasion of one of our rare visits to town. The shops were a glimpse of fairyland and the little money we had so diligently saved put us through agonies of indecision on how best to spend it. The shop keepers of that era gave their customers "Christmas boxes" which included big fruity barm bracks, coloured candles and other goodies. It was a time of plenty but the old and needy were not forgotten and it was the pleasant task of us children to bring a little Christmas cheer into their drab lives.

The puddings would have been made earlier in the month and hung in their floured and greased cloths. Preparing and making them was a pleasant chore and we chopped and stirred and wished with gusto. The postman too was a welcome visitor, and because most people in the area had family in England and America, the registered letters were eagerly looked forward to and were a big help in the lean years of the 1920's.

Christmas cakes as we know them now were unknown except perhaps in the "big houses", but we were lucky. A cousin of my mother's in Kildare sent us an iced cake every Christmas. That cake was the "piece de resistance" of the festivities. We called it the "Kildare Cake'" and talk about it being precious! We each got a slice with lemonade on Christmas Eve while my father had a big glass of punch and wished us go "mbeirimid beo ar an t-am seo aris!" [66]

On Christmas Eve too we put up the decorations – the house had been scrubbed and cleaned on the preceding days. The paper chains and mottoes with Santy's smiling face were put in place and the candles fixed in their decorated containers. We all went to confession and had fish and white sauce for dinner at dusk. At dusk too the candles were lit – to light the Blessed Mother and St Joseph on their journey. We loved going outside to see all the lights in the windows of own and the neighbours' houses.

We went to bed early, full of excitement, having hung our stockings on the chimney place and fearfully willing

---

[66] May we all be alive and well at this time next year.

Santy, or Daddy Christmas as he was then, to visit us. The light was not very bright as we crept downstairs to investigate the contents of the stockings. There was always something nice like a storybook and a coloured hanky, perhaps a little bag of sweets and an apple and orange. So little compared to today, but so much to our simple aspirations.

We went to Mass in the dark. Those were the days before electricity arrived and in the early morning the stars were as bright as they must have been on the first Christmas morning. Neighbours greeted one another "Nollaig shona dhib[67]" and the music of the Adeste (Fidelis) filled the morning air.

Friends and neighbours

A good relationship between neighbours is important in any community, but for farmers in those days it was an absolute necessity.

The system was that everything was shared – horses when needed for ploughing and harvest work, harrows, rollers, hay equipment. The smaller landowners couldn't afford much in the way of working gear but no field was left untilled or no crop unharvested for want of equipment.

But poverty was rampant and how families managed to survive with so little of the world's goods gets more mysterious the more I think back. It was quite usual to rear big families in one-roomed thatched cabins. I can recall one family who lived near us: father, mother and seven children. All father possessed was part ownership of a four-oar boat and even though the fishing season was longer then owing to good summers, there was always the long winter and spring to provide for. It was customary

---

[67] Happy Christmas to you all.

too for farmers to give a few drills of potatoes to landless families in exchange for help at busy times, and there was always the jug of milk and bit of brown flour for the needy.

My favourite couple to visit were Dan and Mag. They were all right financially because they both had the pension, £1 weekly. I loved going down the road with the jug of milk and sometimes I got 2 pence, which was bliss and the reason, no doubt, for my eagerness to visit. Mag was unique, she kept hens and I declare to goodness she could reel off the pedigree of each of them almost like Herd Book cows nowadays. They had a cat called Cluasac and a little dog, Prince. Cluasac was partial to tender young chick and was in constant trouble. Mag had a dresser filled with magnificent china. When making tea she boiled it in a can at the side of the fire. It was so strong it could almost stand on its own, but if one was lucky enough to call on a Friday evening when Dan, and Kruger the donkey, brought the shopping, and Mag cut a big thick slice of fresh crusty bread and home-made butter, that was something worth having.

On Sunday afternoons, I usually went to a nearby house to play with the girls of the family. The mother, God love her, was crippled with arthritis and could only sit and "blow" the fire machine with difficulty. She was an avid reader and had been in America before she married. A relation sent her books and she could tell the stories she had read better that any TV critic. I can remember sitting around the fire on cold Sunday afternoons and listening with rapt attention to tales of East Lynne and such like, while Mary, the eldest girl, who had to take her mother's place at an early age, baked a currant cake for the tea in the bastible. Happy days when our limited horizons did not inhibit us! We were content in our naivety.

The Attridge family lived in the "Tower", a tall slate building on the highest point of the parish with a view of the coastline from Galley head to Kinsale. He was a Coastguard during the last years of British occupation and continued to live in the Tower after the Free State was founded. The "lookout" on the outside of the building was the joy of our young lives and on our return journey from school we often climbed the twenty steps to the top. It was a worthwhile climb – the panoramic spread of sea and countryside was breath taking. Mr Attridge pointed out interesting places and told us about the day the Lusitania[68] was sunk almost straight opposite the Tower. He was a keen gardener and often gave us some of his lovely ripe gooseberries and apples. He was also a great reader and his sons in England sent him the "Daily Mail", which he always passed on to my father. We always looked up to him as the kind cultured gentleman he was.

Memories, Memories

I can remember life even before the pony and trap when we went to mass in the horse and cart. There was a nice bed of straw laid in the bottom of the cart and a big sack filled with straw to sit on. Along with the fact that the cartwheels were iron shod and that the roads were only dirt tracks sheeted with small stones broken with a hammer by the County Council workers, it was anything but a smooth ride. It was a few years on before we got the trap with rubber tyred wheels and much more comfort.

Miss Galwey, who lived on one of the big houses rode in style in a covered car with the driver sitting on a high seat outside. Then came the first motor, owned by Colonel Longfield who lived in Dunowen House. That created some stir in the neighbourhood. Earlier on Lord Carbery of Castlefreke, on the far side of the parish terrified the

---

[68] On May 7, 1915, the British passenger ship was sunk by a German U-boat.

citizens when he drove round the narrow roads. They called his car the "headless coach" and jumped over the fences when they met him.

I saw the first bus when I was about nine years old. It came from Cork on an excursion to Dunnycove Regatta and was the subject of so much interest that the regatta was ignored.

It was as all so very long ago in another life and another culture, but the winds of change were blowing across the Atlantic and a new way of life was gradually transforming the old pattern. The old neighbours were slowly passing away and many of the cabins were empty and falling apart. The district was poorer for their passing. They had all made their mark on the quality of country life.

1934

The second phase of my life meant the ending of National School, passing the Primary Exam, and going on to Secondary. Secondary School was known then as "Secondary Top" and it meant cycling six miles each way to the Convent of Mary in Clonakilty town. The transition was traumatic. Living as we did so far from the town at the very end of the Parish, I had rarely seen a nun and the huge classrooms and equally big classes were overwhelming in the extreme. Bicycles in the 1930's were luxury items and needless to say I did not possess one, but getting to Clonakilty meant I had to have one. So, with great excitement on my part and with much saving and scrimping on my parents I was the proud owner of a new bike. It was an Elswich complete with carrier, for my books, and cost £15: a lot of money in the 1930's.

On my first day, I was put through an extreme exam together with about 12 more country girls. The town girls who had been through Convent Primary were very slick and I'm sure laughed behind their hands at the "country cawbogues."[69]

The number of books was huge, as was the amount of work and I can still remember the first poem we had to learn off by heart in those days: the "Burial of King Cormac". Long and hard, as well as Irish poetry, Irish and European history, world geography, English grammar and literature and an extra language either French or Latin. Maths was the usual arithmetic, algebra and geometry. It was a formidable timetable, and a long day starting off from home at 8.15 am and getting back at 5 pm. The roads were rough, stony and littered with potholes. Twice a year they were sheeted with small stones and for weeks until they sank in a bit they were a nightmare to cycle over as well as disastrous for tyres. It was some years before steam rolling was introduced to say nothing of tarring.

As well as five full days, we had half day on Saturday when we did drawing and Christian Doctrine. It took a few months and diligent application to get into the routine and a lot of midnight oil was burned to get through the homework.

In the 1930's the State exams were only beginning to be included in the school curriculum and Civil Service, teaching and nursing were about the only careers available for girls. One advantage of secondary school was that with the amount of homework I was not expected to contribute to the evening chores on the farm. While attending primary school there were a thousand jobs after school, in the autumn picking potatoes after the plough, helping my brother to slice mangolds and turnips for the cows, turning the wheel to cut furze for the horses and donkey, feeding the young calves after milking and carting into the house

---

A disparaging term for an uncouth person from the Irish word for "clodhopper" or "clown".

timber blocks which keep the fire going, getting the supper and washing up after in a dish of hot water from the kettle. How we have progressed since, with hot water at the turn of a tap, candles and oil lamps replaced with brilliant lighting and cookers and microwaves replacing the open fire and iron pots.

The summer holidays were eagerly looked forward to. It was so good to not to have to get up for school and any chores that had to be done were so much easier in the lovely long sunny days, where you would not need a coat from May to October.

Too soon September came and off on the road again back to school. The time passed and the knowledge grew, encouraged and helped by the good sisters dedicated to giving young people a future.

I ended up in the Department of Trade and Industry in Dublin's Lord Edward St. I stayed in digs in Drumcondra and I cycled to work across the river. My wages were small and I had to survive on very little. Dublin then was a nice city where it was possible to walk unaccompanied at any time. For a few pennies, it was possible to go on the train to Bray or Howth or any of the interesting suburbs and when funds allowed, a cup of tea and a bun for 6 pennies. In the winter, there was such variety: the cinema, the Abbey and the Gaiety theatres. One could get to "the Gods" (the seats furthest from the stage) for a shilling, and 2 pennies for a packet of sweets. Phoenix Park was a joy, the flowers and shrubs and lovely walks. Croke Park was one shilling and six pence for the side-line.

I remember September 3rd, 1939 when Cork and Kilkenny played the Hurling Final. That morning on the radio the British Prime Minister Chamberlain declared war on Germany. Life for everyone was much harder for the next six years. Most food stuffs were rationed: half an ounce of tea, 2 ounces of sugar only on ration books, no white flour or bread; clothes, candles, oil, all rationed but at least we were not involved in the awful war. Stories of the raid on Britain and of the thousands dead came through on the radio and somehow we kept out of it.

I left Dublin and got married back home in Ardfield: that was now the third phase of my life. I was back to farming, back to my roots. After the war, everything took on a new aspect and in a few years things started to take a new turn. For us country folk the electrification was a red-letter day. The light meant that in winter every farmyard was lighted, milking machines were installed to ease the heavy chore of milking and every hand worked appliance was converted to electricity making life so much easier. Electric pumps brought water up from the depths in every farmyard and along with the "power" tractors were appearing with attachments for all farm work. The days of the horse were fast disappearing, we were on the road to progress both indoors and out.

We had come through some hard times, times when money was scarce and we bartered farm produce for necessities. The country was settling down after years of internal trouble and our standard of living grew with the years, for better or worse, time will tell.

Lightning Strike[70]

The third of February 1963 started off like any other winter morning, dark and drizzly and bitterly cold. The cows were milked and Denny had gone to the creamery. Eileen had gone down to the yard to feed the pigs and attend to her horse. Suddenly, without warning, it got as dark as night and the kitchen was illuminated by what seemed to be a hundred bulbs. At the same moment, the

---

[70] First published in the Ardfield Ratherbarry Journal No 4 2002-2003.

thunder shook the house. That was it – one flash, one unearthly peal of thunder and devastation!

In total shock, I tore out of the house, sure and certain that Eileen must be dead. Thankfully, I met her coming across the yard. She and the dog were in the tractor house when the[71] lightning struck, it made a hole in the ground just feet away from her. The horse had burst out the door and gone wild. When we went into the pigs' house, they were all dead and we didn't see the dogs for days after.

We got ourselves up to the house and it was then that the disaster was evident. Most of the gable wall was blown away. Inside the house the scene was horrendous; every plug and socket was blown out of the walls, the wires torn out of the TV and the phone in the hall was halfway up the stairs.

Our initial reaction was to sit down and burst into tears, but worse was still to come. We hadn't thought of the cows and it wasn't until Denny had come home from the creamery and went into the stall that the final blow struck. Two of the best cows, three-year-old Pedigree Friesians, were dead. Amazingly, another was still alive between them. They had been Denny's pride and joy, and he was grooming one of them for the Dublin Spring Show.

I can only compare the house to a wake-house for the next few days. All the neighbours and friends came to see the damage and to commiserate with us, still in shock. The help and service we got from the builder, the ESB and phone people was beyond words. Pat O'Sullivan came from Clonakilty with a team of men and material and they did a terrific job on the gable. The ESB worked all day and into the night and brought back power, and we had the phone a few days later.

---

[71] Eileen was about twenty years old at the time and says that she thinks the Wellington boots she was wearing saved her.

But the psychological effect of the whole disaster was phenomenal. It took a long time to come to terms with what, was in hindsight, our Armageddon. Even today, fifty years on, I still feel physically sick when there is thunder or lightning, and I live again through that morning in 1963.

"Women of Ireland, always behind their men no matter what the cost to themselves. Glorious unsung heroines ready to give and not to count the cost, to labour and not heed the wounds, always doing their duty as they saw it, with very little reward." Margaret Feen

In her own hand:

After the war everything took on a new aspect. In a few years everything started to take a good turn. For us country folk the Rural Electrification was red letter. The poles were up all over West Cork and the light & power came on and changed the face of the country and the lives of the people. The light meant that in the winter every yard was lighted, milking machines were installed to ease the heavy chore of milking – every hand worked appliance was connected to electricity making life so much easier. Electric pumps brought the water up from the depths in every farmyard and along with the power tractors were appearing with attachments for all farm work. The days of the horse were fast disappearing. – we were on the road to progress both indoors and out.

We had come through some hard times, times when money was scarce and we

****

Impressions of Clonakilty in 1998

My husband collected us from Cork airport on the last Saturday of March 1998 after 24 hours travelling from New Zealand. Our daughter and I had never visited Ireland and it was to be our new home for at least four years. We knew no one who lived there and unlike some of our friends in New Zealand, had no Irish heritage. It was a cold dark day with rain threatening and the leafless trees along the muddy roadside were flapping in places with wind-trapped plastic bags. But we felt happy and optimistic about the new adventure we were about to begin.

It didn't take long to reach Clonakilty as there was little traffic on the winding narrow road that cut through the fields. My husband, whose job had brought us to Ireland, had already set up a temporary home for us in the West Cork Holiday Homes, new gaily painted terraced houses on the bay end of the town. Before taking us there he wanted to drive us down the main street. I was aghast when he approached the An Sugan on Ashe Street, "Stop! Surely this can't be a two-way street, it is so narrow!" But it was back then.

The next day, Sunday, we decided to drive to Cork City to purchase a few household items. Our container from NZ wouldn't be delivered for some months. We had difficulty finding shops open in the Central city, Dunnes at Bishopstown being the only one.

On Monday my husband, our fifteen-year-old daughter and I began exploring Clonakilty together. The brightly decorated shop fronts with their intricate and striking Irish signage were delightful. "Lovely day" most of the shopkeepers said to us. We were mystified, as it was the sort of day everyone in New Zealand complained about and called "cold and bleak". But we became aware that it wasn't raining or windy. We were surprised that many of the shops and businesses opened at 10am and closed at 1pm for dinner hour, but liked the way they stayed open until 6pm. Later we discovered Wednesday all-day shop closure was common, but Saturday openings were great.

We began to settle in. The pace of life was slow enough that people stopped their cars when passing in different directions on the main street and wound down their windows to have a chat. To me the streets seemed to ring with the musical sound of women's voices calling out cheerfully, "Hello, how are ye?" to each other. The bus to and from the west sometimes caused traffic jams when it went through Pearse Street. Cars were allowed to park facing in either direction parallel to the roadside, regardless of the direction in which they are travelling. The number of vehicles was fewer than we expected with many small Ford Fiestas. Some older farmers drove to Mass leaving their tractors parked on the edge of town. There was periodic ringing of the Catholic Church bells throughout the day, and people paused to make the sign of the cross. It was rare to see someone of different ethnicity on the streets: almost everyone was Irish.

Over the following weeks we sorted out many things. We had the telephone connected but had to pay a 100 Irish pounds bond, to be repaid after one year, because we weren't Irish. We visited all the high schools that took girls in Bandon and Clonakilty. Our daughter chose Sacred Heart in Clonakilty as the one she liked the best. A school that was very friendly and welcoming, the teachers were not all female, and they were prepared to help her catch up with her lack of a foreign language. It was a great choice, but quite an ambitious one: she wasn't used to single-sex education, religious instruction, a school uniform and a largely mono-cultural population but she thrived on the experience. However, the biggest plus was that we consequently chose Clonakilty as our hometown. We can hardly believe our luck now, to be part of such a close, vibrant and progressive community. We began seeking a house to buy in or near Clonakilty. After being shown the half dozen available, none of which were suitable, our spirits began to fall. However, I was delighted when the last auctioneer in town told me he knew of a house under construction.

We felt instantly at home in Redwood Park. It was set in Barry Shanahan's former tree nursery and many of the mature trees were familiar NZ native ones. At that time Tawnies Grove and Gravel Pit Lane, which led from the Western Road to Redwood Park, were bounded on both sides by stone walls and for some distance the Lane was paved with cobbles. After passing Ard Charraig, the grassy Parish Field lay on the northern side. A horse grazed there picturesquely against a backdrop of flowering hawthorns and poplars.

The house deal was sealed with a handshake and we were asked to choose fixtures and fittings the very next day. The papers were signed nine weeks later, the week before we moved in. Meanwhile, we had to learn a whole new language having never used terms like press (cupboard), guttering (spouting), and rads (radiators, not usually present in a NZ home) to explain our requirements. Our builder was somewhat mystified when we said we needed four hotpoints (electrical outlets) in every room, as Hotpoint is an appliance brand in Ireland. Due to the rich West Cork accent, when the Irish men were speaking with each other we had no idea of what they were saying, but it was easier if they were speaking only to us.

Buying a new house was a big help to settling in because it came with 14 new neighbours, with all of whom we had things in common: the same builder and and a similar house. It was useful for future maintenance in that we got to know all the tradesmen who worked on the house. When the Good Friday Agreement was signed in 1998 as part of the Northern Ireland peace process, the men spontaneously documented it on a rafter in our attic to commemorate the occasion.

Many of us in the Park were also new to Clonakilty. It was a surprise to learn that residents from Skibbereen were considered "Blow-ins"[72] too. I was greeted with a friendly handshake from both men and women and the phrase, "You are very welcome to Ireland, Alison". The use of names in casual speech being charmingly more frequent on an everyday basis than in our homeland.

It was usually assumed that we were Australian. Not everyone could understand what we were saying and in these circumstances, we could not usually understand everything they were saying either. We went to purchase a car for me: I had never driven anything other than automatic transmission. We were advised that automatics were in short supply as they were not popular, and we were directed to the Toyota Dealership in Macroom. I could barely understand the salesman and no doubt the feeling was mutual. My husband said to me, "Don't be surprised if they tell you the car was previously owned by a "priest's housekeeper", as this was something he had experienced a few times. However, the one I chose was, "previously owned by the Reverend Mother". Getting to Macroom and back was a navigational challenge when there were few road signs, and because of the round poles they were attached to, some could be pointing in the opposite direction to the correct one.

Having lived in upstate New York in my early 20's I thought that it would be easy to settle into Irish life. But

---

[72] Outsiders or foreigners.

the cultural gap was much wider. The major difference was that most people stayed up very late at night, which we were unused to. However, the positive flip side was the late start in the morning. You could be sure that unexpected callers would not come before 11am. Tea breaks and lunch times were an hour later than in NZ or US. Most people ate their main meal of the day at 1pm, so were not that interested in coming to our home for dinner at 7pm. The word "afternoon" was seldom heard and instead "evening" seemed to begin after 2pm and stretch until bedtime.

On weekends, we explored the area by car and were delighted by the profusion of wild primroses and violets on the ditches, the name for the vegetation covered stone walls lining the rural roads. Enjoying the glory of carpets of bluebells in the Courtmacsherry and Castlefreke woods was divine, as deciduous woods don't exist in NZ nature. We wondered why so many cars were muddied almost up to the door handles and learned that the winter harvest of sugar beet caused agricultural vehicles to transfer mud onto the country roads. The distinctive smell of slurry was also new, as indoor housing of animals was rare in New Zealand. Occasionally we saw settlements of Irish Travellers in caravans and trailer homes parked on the side of the road at Red Strand and in a layby on the road to Bandon. We got used to the sonic boom created by the nightly traverse of the Concorde plane over Ireland en route from Paris to New York.

As with most people in a new place we wondered how well we were going to manage on only one salary in Irish pounds. We were puzzled that newspapers did not run advertisements for home appliances and groceries. With a new house and lifestyle, I was relying on them to figure out the best prices for household chattels. I learned that the weekly Southern Star was the paper to read for local news, and although the most "positive news" newspaper we have ever read, it carried no advertising either. So, I "shopped around" by telephone for large electrical appliances, but I soon realised that I was easily identified by my accent and it wasn't a common thing to do, so quit.

One Wednesday while walking dreamily between the Library and the Post Office I experienced one of the most alarming moments in my life. I turned the corner into Bridge St and came face to face with an armed soldier in camouflage uniform pointing his gun at me! Other soldiers were nearby. My brain whirled as I tried to figure out what could be happening and I backed away in shock. I learned it was the regular weekly uplifting of the money from the banks and Post Office with an Army escort in a convoy of vehicles. Instances of IRA robberies had made this necessary in the Republic.

My husband's specialist skills enabled his employer to obtain a work permit for him. As a non-EU resident, my passport was stamped disallowing any form of work or business employment for me. We all had to report to the Gardae on a regular basis to have our Alien's Residency Card stamped in a little grey cardboard booklet. In 1998, it seemed it was rare for people to be moving to Ireland and there were no visas for us. In order for our daughter and me to gain entrance to Ireland we had to carry a copy of a letter of employment for my husband. It had been faxed and photocopied so many times that his picture was only just recognisable. Some years later, we became Irish Citizens, my husband first, in Bandon. My turn came a year or so later. I had to swear fidelity to the Irish nation in the Clonakilty courthouse in the company of a large number of people, publicans seeking dance licences and a prisoner handcuffed to a Garda. Later, in the post we received attractive laminated A4 certificates, which we assumed attested to our new status. They were in the Irish language and the only words we recognised were our names and birth-dates.

Supervalu was the biggest and most modern super-market in town, although only a fraction of its current size. After we moved to Redwood Park I would drive there to shop at around 3 pm and our daughter would walk from school and meet me in the aisles. The selection of fruits (mainly apples, oranges, and bananas) and vegetables (mainly potatoes, onions, carrots, leeks, cabbages, and turnips) was very basic. I love to bake and wasn't aware such tiny tins of baking powder and golden syrup existed. Trips to Bandon were necessary to find whole dried dates. On the other hand, I had never seen the variety and types of cut of bacon for boiling and did not know how to use them. Once plain cooked white rice was being promoted in Super Valu for people to taste.

Then it was necessary to go to Cork about once a month to buy specialty food items we used frequently, like soy sauce, clothing for tall women and girls and home décor items. Supervalu, the largest supermarket in town then, also gave out tokens, according to the money spent on groceries, to redeem in store. Items of furniture at minimal cost came in rotation; sturdy chests of wooden drawers, bedside cabinets, bookcases, garden and rocking chairs, rugs and lamps. They were very popular. As was the most generous Christmas gift of a calendar and a Christmas cake for every customer.

One unexpected thing it took me ages to learn was how to make mashed potatoes in Ireland. It was something I learned at my mother's. You peeled the potatoes, put them in a pot with a little salt, covered them with water, and brought them to the boil. When fork tender you drained them, added a knob of butter and a little milk and mashed them. Every time I tried in Clonakilty they turned into potato soup. It was a very long time after, that I learned that the Irish potatoes available at the time, were different and best boiled or steamed with the skins on and peeled and mashed after cooking.

In 1998, we seldom saw children playing outdoors with skateboards, bikes, toys or pets. Clonakilty did not have a children's playground then. There was no movie theatre at the time, although these things quickly changed with the new prosperity brought by The Celtic Tiger economy[73]. Town and country dwellers towing trailers or boats for recreational purposes were very rare.

In 1998, we had two glorious weeks of summer in May. We realised why so many people made the most of it, as it turned out to be the only long period of sunny days we had that year. There was no summer school-uniform and summer clothing was referred to as "holiday clothes". We had not heard the term "sun holiday" as our summer was always a time of too much sun, "Slip, slop, slap", was the motto down-under: slip on a shirt, slop on some sunscreen and slap on a hat. In Clonakilty, a suntan was prized amongst women and girls and make-up, artificial tans, sunbeds and holidays in sunny climes were often used to achieve it.

One of the first challenges I faced was how I could become part of the local community. My husband had his job and our daughter school, but with no job allowed, and no interest in pursuing sport I had to make my own way. A friendly neighbour and I did some courses in Clonakilty and Cork together, but the breakthrough came thanks to Kate Coveney and the Clonakilty Library. I asked if they knew of a Book Discussion Group I could join. They did not, but Kate said that if I wished to start one, they would

---

[73] Wikipedia: "The Irish economy expanded at an average rate of 9.4% between 1995 and 2000 and continued to grow at an average rate of 5.9% during the following decade until 2008, when it fell into recession."

help by providing the library books, venue and morning tea. An advertisement in the Southern Star drew a crowd to the first meeting on November the 11th, 1998 and this became a wonderful avenue to meet like-minded people. Sometime later a Writer's Group also grew out of the interest in books and both groups still meet.

Living in Ireland made us realise that New Zealand, even though it is a very new country in comparison, did have its own culture. Our homes are a big part of who we are. We like to show people around new houses because most people are interested; we entertained at home more than in public places; we could have a good time without lots of live music or drink. We spend a lot of time outside. We love to do home improvement projects, like making and maintaining flower and vegetable gardens, building things, cleaning cars and windows and having shared barbeques. Most of us participate in some sort of sport or outdoor activity and the beach is the popular Christmas holiday spot.

In contrast, due to the climate, many Irish fun times took place indoors then. Back in the late nineteen-nineties we learned it was rude to arrive on time to someone's home if you were invited. If a cup of tea or something to eat was offered to a West Cork person they often politely declined. It was only later, to my distress that I learned this was polite behaviour and you were to put the kettle on anyway, encouraging with a quick "Ah, go-on, go-on". Also, in contrast to NZ, we learned that farmers did not like to be asked how many cows or acres they had, because it was considered private information.

We loved the neighbourly conviviality of the cold wintertime Irish Christmas. Short days where the decorated and brightly lit shops are inviting and a home-made Christmas wreath looks fresh on the front door for a month. And what fun it is to pick the holly and ivy from

206

one's own garden. A huge contrast to Christmas shopping in the bright sun and sticky heat with the Christmas lights not visible until 9pm.

Our passion for Clonakilty is huge after nearly 20 years living here, albeit for only half the year now. We quickly came to love all the differences of our adopted hometown and the safe and pleasant lifestyle it offers. We've learned a lot about the history that made life so difficult in Ireland for so long. The stable, close-knit community of locals plus the enthusiastic energy of blow-ins and the caring for those less fortunate is appreciated. A rich local culture is retained due to the many talented musicians, writers and artists. Summer festivals, multiple different interest groups, and the vibrant and friendly shopping community (including the weekly market on Fridays) make it popular with holiday-makers, along with the stunning beauty of the coast and countryside. The pace of life is slower but every modern amenity is here to keep in touch with the wider world.

We have seen huge changes in the town and lifestyle since those days in 1998, but Clonakilty retains its quintessential small town, big heart feel. We will always love it as much as our original homeland.

****

Rites of Passage

The following sections deal with common experiences of many local women in the twentieth century.

Birth

During the first half of the twentieth century babies were most commonly born at home with a doctor or midwife in attendance. The baby's abdomen was commonly bound with a strip of linen to protect the umbilicus and prevent herniation. Mothers were advised to spend ten days in bed afterwards, a practice that was abandoned later in the century when prolonged bed rest was known to increase complications like deep vein thrombosis. Mothers fed their own babies from the breast normally until the child was about a year old and sometimes supplemented that with a bread, milk and sugar mixture known as "goody" until the baby was weaned gradually and began to eat normal food.

The baby clothes were hand made by knitting or hand sewing in most cases. Diapers were made from old sheets or flour bags in the early half of the century, and later from towelling squares, fastened with a safety pin. In those days, many future mothers learned their childcare skills from caring for younger siblings.

Women had to be "churched" before they could return to Mass. The following article explains the custom.

"Incredible as it may seem now, until the 1960s, many women who gave birth could only return to the church after they received a blessing from a priest. This 'churching' took place five or six weeks after the birth purportedly so that the 'sin of childbirth' could be washed away [74]. Thus, the mother was not present at the

---

[74] Irish Independent 13 December 2012, "Churching, labour and deliveries."

christening."

In the 1960's the Second Vatican Council introduced a funeral rite for babies who died before baptism. This ended the heart-breaking practice of them being buried outside the graveyard, in non-consecrated ground. Up until the 1970's it was also not uncommon for the Priest to veto the parents' wishes for baby names and the names of saints or biblical references given preference.

Until late in the mid-century it was an expectation of many men, and the church, that a woman's role was to produce a baby every year. This practice took its toll on the health of both mother and child although some found creative ways around this.

Unmarried motherhood was considered socially unacceptable and girls were either sent to England if it could be afforded, or to the infamous Magdalene Laundries, where the girls were forced to earn their keep by working for up to two years after the birth. Their babies were adopted and often went overseas. Abortion is still illegal in Ireland. Up until the 1960's it could be very hard for rural childless couples because their own parents might veto adoption, if a farm was likely to be inherited.

In the second half of the century it gradually became more common for mothers to travel to nursing homes or hospital for the birth. In line with modern trends the lying-in time was reduced dramatically; medical and surgical labour interventions became more common and breast-feeding dwindled for some time.

Marriage

While many people met and married for love, matches were still made for some rural couples up until the 1950's, especially if land was involved. Special "matchmakers" would be employed to find a suitable spouse. The custom of a dowry being paid when a girl married, also persisted in some farming families. Part of the dowry paid would be used to assist in providing dowries for the bridegroom's sisters. There was a saying that, "One dowry could marry a whole county".

Most often church weddings were held in the morning and the couple would go away for a short holiday (if they could afford it) following a wedding breakfast with close friends and family in a local hotel or sometimes at home. Wedding clothes were most often those that could be used in the future for best, because materials were often in short supply due to war and/or economic reality. The "white weddings" of today were an innovation made fashionable by Queen Victoria and were not practical for most until later in the 20th century.

Should the marriage not be a happy one, divorce was not an option until 1996. For many a rural woman marriage meant moving from her father's house to her husband's house, the only two homes she would ever know. However, rural Ireland had, and still has an unusually high number of people who, for lack of opportunity or the wish to, chose never to marry.

Death

Many of the traditions associated with death are still observed today. Although now it would be more usual for the laying out to be carried out by an undertaker, rather than the local nurse or midwife, some people both in town and country are still waked at home. The tradition of a person being laid out in a simple "brown habit" persisted until around the 1950's but had fallen away in most instances later. The brown habit was thought to bring to the wearer special indulgences (such as less time spent in purgatory) if blessed by a priest with the dying person's hand resting in the habit.

In the traditional wake the clocks in the house were stopped at the hour of death and mirrors covered to protect against the effect of old superstitions that would bode ill for both the dead and the living. Special white embroidered or lace embellished bed linens would be used to dress the bed on which the body lay. Five candles, representing the five senses would be lit on a white draped table at the bedside, on which a crucifix and holy water would be placed. Neighbours and friends would come to the house to say the rosary and pay their respects and many would sit up with the family all night (and sometimes for several days) to ensure the person was definitely dead before they were buried. Much drinking of poitin[75] or whiskey and reminiscing would go on. Often in rural areas the funeral mass would be said by the Priest in the home and the body taken directly to the graveyard.

Undertakers and funeral directors took over many of the practical functions of coping with the dead in the Clonakilty area, after the mid twentieth century. Rooms were provided where those affected by the death could come to express their condolences to the family and say goodbye to the body in the open coffin. The rosary would be said and the removal of the body from the funeral home to the church the night before the funeral became common practice. Notifications of deaths are announced daily on local radio. Following the funeral, burial in the local graveyard is still the norm [76] and it is quite common for the distance from church to graveyard to be walked

---

[75] Highly alcoholic distilled beverage.

[76] The old practice of burying unbaptized people, suicides, criminals and strangers at crossroads or in unconsecrated ground has been abandoned.

alongside the hearse. Special masses are held on dates one month and one year after the death.

Becoming a woman, wife & mother.

Most of the women I spoke to who grew up in the 1900's had little prior knowledge of what was happening to them at the time of the onset of menstruation and/or married life. For women born in the latter half of the century, books and sometimes ante-natal education were available, but were not always easily accessible. Living in a rural district, rather than a city, perhaps made it more difficult. Mothers did not seem to pass on very much information in either regard.

Due to the strong Catholic ethos in Ireland there has been a great reluctance in many schools to take up the initial 1997 Irish Government guidelines proposal for Relationships and Sexuality education (RSE) and it was left to schools to decide if it "fitted with their ethos". As recently as May 18, 2015 the Irish Times featured the following headline and banner: "Sex ed. in Ireland: 'It's all disease, risk and crisis pregnancy'. Sex education in Irish schools is patchy and often concentrates on the negative aspects. In this environment, parents should step in and talk to their children about sex, early and often". Schools are still free to deliver RSE according to their ethos, with some opting for abstinence-only models and others offering a more comprehensive programme. Schools can, and many do, ignore the advice of the Department of Education. The area remains one of the most contentious aspects of the second-level curriculum." When one girl was 15 she asked her older married sister, "Is it out of your belly button that the baby came?"

Experiences of two girls in the 1960's.

Girl A: There was no sex education when I was at school. I think it has only been part of the curriculum since about the year 2000. I was kept very innocent of everything. When I got my first period my mother got the necessary supplies for me and I was told, "Don't let anyone touch you now".

Girl B: I started to menstruate at fourteen, a time when my mother was too ill to ask her about it. Having never been told, I didn't know what was happening to me, or how to deal with it. My aunt explained to me what to do. I had to purchase "women's things" from the Co-op store. In those days, they were uncomfortable and not very effective pads with loops fastening them to an elastic band worn around the waist. Girls had to soak their underwear in salted water to get rid of the stains. Worse, the package of "women's things" was never wrapped and you had to walk out with them in your hands: so embarrassing! I was taught that from now on I was to be very careful of men and boys and never to let them touch me below the waist. Sex education at school had not been put in place in the 1970's and so I learned about the facts of life from my husband.

Childbirth experiences

Woman A: When I had my first child in the 1990's, my husband never accompanied me to the dozen or so antenatal classes. I was uncomfortable being the odd one out and didn't complete them all. So after a tiny bleed, I went into St Finbarr's hospital in Cork at about 10am thinking I was in labour. In retrospect, I should have stayed at home for much longer. At the time, my specialist was doing his hospital rounds. As I was a private patient, without consultation, he put me onto a drip to hasten delivery. It gave me horrendous labour pains and I was in agony. The gas and air I was given did not work. I laboured away in a room with two other patients. My husband made a brief appearance but the Dr told the nurse to, "Take him out of the room as he is doing no good to the patient".

I was pleased to be able to breast-feed my baby girl for the first three months of her life. I did not go back to that Doctor for my second pregnancy. Midwives delivered my second baby and I could visualise the different chapters of the textbook I had read about labour and delivery as I went through them. Both babies were delivered while I was on my back with my legs held out of the way in stirrups.

Woman B: When I became pregnant with my only child in the 1980's I knew that nature would take care of the baby being born and I wasn't too keen to know the details of how that happened. Although I read my books about maternity and childcare avidly, I avoided the pages about labour. I had just one scan early in my pregnancy and was told all was as it should be. The first sign I had that I was in labour was bleeding and lots of it, starting in the night. I thought it was my waters breaking, so I happily perched on the toilet with my contractions thinking how wonderful it was that my precious baby was soon to be born. Thankfully my younger sister realised that this was not normal and phoned the St Finbarr's Hospital in Cork and they immediately sent an ambulance. I probably should have had a Caesarean section, but after labouring away for hours my baby was finally safely delivered. Meanwhile I had lost a great deal of blood, received many blood transfusions and took two weeks to recover well enough to be sent home. However, I am proud that I managed to breastfeed my baby, despite some difficulties, and kept it up for ten months giving her the best possible new beginning. Breastfeeding was not widely approved of and viewed as somehow unseemly, even by other women, despite being done with great discretion.

Managing a smaller family size?

This was the question I posed to a number of women as contraceptive devices could legally be used, but not sold or imported into the Republic of Ireland between 1935 and 1980[77]. The Papal encyclical Humanae vitae (1968) also decreed that artificial contraception in all forms was immoral. These were the answers I was given:

- Housework or cooking late into the night until "himself was asleep" was effective for some.
- There was very little sex before marriage as most girls were very frightened of shaming the family by becoming pregnant before marriage. The Magdalene Laundries[78] fearsome reputation added to this.
- Some women deliberately married at a later age so that they were less fertile, to avoid a big family.
- Some "had the grand feel". In other words, they thought that they were superior and presumably were able to source contraceptives from Northern Ireland, or abstained. A small family was often considered as "a gentleman's family". The more affluent could take the train to Northern Ireland or go to England for a supply of contraceptives.
- The husband sometimes worked away from home or was at sea for part of the year.
- One person, presumably using the rhythm method of birth control, reported that she tapped her husband's back if it was the right night for love.

---

[77] https://en.wikipedia.org/wiki/Contraception_in_the_Republic_of_Ireland
[78] https://en.wikipedia.org/wiki/Magdalene_asylum

- But for many women the situation was that "the husband hopped on and hopped off" and a baby arrived nine months later".

Maternity care in the 1990's
By a local midwife and mother.

Most Clonakilty women went to the Cork hospitals of Erinville, Bon Secours or St Finbarr's to have their babies in the 1990's. Times were changing although the Catholic Church was still in charge of decisions regarding the "unborn child" healthy or not. In the 21st Century, the Government now has more say on the matter. Abortions, on any grounds, were banned and still are at the time of writing. Many unfortunate girls were forced to go to England in secret to avail of the service. I also recall baptising a full-term child: the poor baby was not developed for survival. Sadly, the mother was aware of this throughout her pregnancy but she was forced to go to full term and deliver her baby, as there was no other alternative.

In the 1990's all women were encouraged to take advantage of prenatal care that was provided free of charge for those who went to public hospitals. If private maternity care had been chosen, the patient paid for private pre-natal classes. Once mother and baby returned home the Public Health nurses called regularly over the first few weeks to check the baby was feeding well and gaining weight. They gave advice where help was needed and reinforced the benefits of mother regularly doing exercises to strengthen pelvic floor muscles. After that, mother and baby attended a local clinic for check-up and vaccinations. Six weeks after the birth the mother would return to hospital, or her specialist, for a check on her own condition.

There was a big emphasis on pain relief during labour. Nitrous oxide and air could be self-administered by the mother via a mask and a form of local anaesthesia called an epidural, administered by injection into the spinal cord, was strongly recommended. The father of the baby was allowed to be in the room to support the baby's mother at the birth, including at Caesarean Sections. In a normal hospital delivery, the mother lay on her back with her feet in stirrups, but in the 1990's a new trend to test different ways of birthing were investigated, including the mother lying on her side or squatting, or giving birth in a specially designed birthing bath of warm water. Home deliveries were also beginning to become popular again.

Breast-feeding was really encouraged for its health benefits to both mother and baby using the slogan "Breast is Best". Babies were kept in the nursery on the first day and night after delivery, with mothers encouraged to feed them. On following days, the baby would be with its mother during the day and go the nursery only at night to assist the mother being rested on discharge. Most women were discharged on day three or four after the heel prick test. "Newborn screening for Phenylketonuria (PKU) [via a drop of blood taken by heel prick] started in Ireland in February 1966. Ireland was one of the first countries in the world to have a national screening programme. Since then [seven] other [serious but treatable] conditions have been added, including Cystic Fibrosis in July 2011. More conditions will be added in the future."[79]

****

---

79 From Health Services Website: Website: hse.ie

An Teach Beag at night, one of Clonakilty and Ireland's most
photographed pubs.

The Role of the ICA

"The Irish Countrywomen's Association (ICA) began in 1910 as a non-denominational and non-party political movement called the United Irishwomen (UI) founded by Mrs Harold Lett. Its aim was to "To improve the standard of life in rural Ireland through Education and Co-operative effort". Sir Horace Plunkett, the founder of the Irish Cooperative movement, influenced its ethos and saw women as the key to realising his movement's aims of better living for farm families.

Up to this point in time rural women had lives epitomized by exhausting work and privation They had neither a vote, nor social life, nor anything to call their own. It was considered a radical idea to encourage women to go out of their homes and priests were reported as saying that, "Women should stay at home and look after their husbands and children and not be going out to meetings".

According to the ICA website[80] "In the early days of the United Irishwomen, potatoes, cabbage and onions were about all the vegetables most people grew and ate. The UI bought a wider variety of seeds and encouraged women to grow a bigger variety of vegetables and special vegetable cookery classes were organised. They also started gardens in schools. As the membership grew, advice was also given on poultry and egg production, cow-testing, cheese making, and bee-keeping, and these initiatives resulted in better diet and nutrition and therefore improved health. One of the other results was the opportunity for women to generate their own income from selling the surplus products."

---

[80] www.ica.ie

The organisation changed its name to the ICA in 1935 and at around the same time, guilds were started up in towns as well.

In the 1950's electricity and safe running water were identified by the ICA as key amenities to achieve the Co-operative movement's aims of better living. The ICA initiated a campaign urging rural women not to marry a farmer unless he supplied running water in his house as well as his byre. As it says on the website: "He thought it a fine idea to put it into his byre, but 'why would you be bothered putting it into the kitchen – wasn't she well fit to carry a few buckets?' [was the] sort of attitude." An ICA poster of the time depicted two women carrying buckets. The slogan read, "We did not promise to love, honour and carry water". In 1958 an ICA/ESB "Model Farm Electrical Kitchen" was constructed and then displayed around the country to demonstrate the ideal possible.

The ICA also made other huge contributions to women's health, welfare, and economic security, in part through adult education via summer schools. According to a letter and story published in the Ardfield/Rathbarry Journal[81] a Summer Camp was held for members of the ICA in the unfurnished Castlefreke in 1934. It was reported that the Castle was in good order, but members had to bring their own bag to fill with straw as there were no beds. Members came from all over bringing food for the kitchen in the form of eggs, chickens, butter, potatoes and so on. Learning new crafts, listening to talks, singing, dancing and drama filled their days. The summer schools were held throughout the Second World War in vacant schools or empty houses until the ICA's An Grianàn college was established in 1954.

---

[81] Ardfield/Rathbarry Journal No.4 2002-03, page 71

The ICA also encouraged rural tourism, Irish culture, arts and crafts, and established the Irish Country markets and the young people's organization, Foroige, amongst many other accomplishments. The ICA is still active today in the greater Clonakilty area.

Clonakilty women at the ICA College, An Grianàn

Women, tea, soda bread & scones

Tea making and its consumption became a bigger part of the lives of the women in Ireland after World War 2 when tealeaves became more widely available and less expensive. It was the drink of choice for women and a great thirst quencher for anyone expending a lot of energy working. The tea was (and is) nearly always served strong to ensure the flavour was not dampened by added milk. In the early days milk was added to keep the cost of the drink down and it became the widespread custom. Today the Republic of Ireland is said to be the biggest consumer of black tea leaves in the world and the Irish Barry's or Lyon's tea always make most welcome gifts to members of the Irish diaspora.

Irish soda bread is as ubiquitous and delicious as tea. It consists simply of brown or white flour, salt, sour milk or buttermilk and baking soda. This can be assembled quickly (as it does not require kneading) and was baked as a round cake, sometimes marked into four quarters, in a bastible over a fire before electricity, or as a cake or loaf in a tin in the oven since. Irish butter is liberally applied to each slice when cool.

The Irish traditional bread rises exclusively with Bread Soda, otherwise known as baking soda, or bicarbonate of soda. The question arises as to why this is so, and why yeast was not used as is customary in so many other places. The answer lies in the low protein composition of Irish grown wheat due to the cool damp climate.

High gluten content is required for yeast to work. The characteristic light but chewy texture is formed when gluten in bread dough forms stretchy cells that expand to hold the gases produced by yeast. However, Irish wheat rises when lactic acid in the milk interacts with bicarbonate of soda to form tiny bubbles of carbon dioxide. It is thought that bicarbonate of soda was introduced to Ireland around the 1840's.

Scones are as popular as soda bread, and are usually made with white flour and baking powder. Sometimes dried fruit is added or wholemeal flour used.

Recipe for Tea Scones
    230 grams flour
    60 grams butter
    30 grams castor sugar
    ¼ teaspoon salt
    1 teaspoon baking powder
    1 beaten egg
    About 100mls milk

Heat oven to 220 C. Sieve dry ingredients into a bowl. Rub finely chopped butter into dry ingredients. Add wet ingredients into dry and mix lightly. Lightly roll out dough and cut into squares or rounds. Brush tops with milk. Bake for 10 minutes until light brown. Split and serve warm with butter, cream or cream cheese, and raspberry jam. Makes six delicious 70mm round scones.

Adapted from "All in the Cooking"

Cash's General Drapery

Most Clonakilty people would have crossed the threshold of Cash's, a general drapery store, for many reasons over the years. It has been outfitting the town for generations. Cash's is a unique store that retains a lot of old world charm and will surprise you with the bounteous stock and excellent selection that it carries.

Cash's daily ledger books date back to 1885. Jeremiah Collins opened this stand-alone business at 25 Rossa Street, where it remains today. Legend has it that Jeremiah was known as "Ready Cash" and that is where the name "Cash's" came from. It is very much a family business and many of the family have worked there through the years. The present General Manager, Mr Des Leader, being a grand-nephew of Jeremiah Collins, and his niece, Mandy who shepherds the staff, is Jeremiah's great grandniece.

Time and the introduction of new materials and ways of doing things have brought about necessary changes in the stock. In the early days, most people were purchasing different types of fabric and the sewing requisites to turn them into useful garments or items for the home or school. Some of the staff remember the addresses and personalities of the tailors and dressmakers in the town that the materials would be delivered to, but now ready-made clothes are the norm. In the past the shop kept a variety of accounts for customers but not as many these days. Packages were always wrapped in brown paper and tied with string.

Tights have replaced suspender belts, and corsets went out of fashion 50 years ago. There was a time when there was a whole wall of selected wool, needles and knitting patterns, but the art of knitting and its necessity for warm garments and socks, is not as commonplace as it used to be. In later years an extensive range of fabrics for curtains has also given way to a large range of readymade ones. Cloth nappies, safety pins and plastic pants were also big sellers until disposable nappies became established. Children's wear gave way to local specialist stores to keep the little ones in fashionable easy-care gear.

Surprising items that there is still a demand for are, Interlock knickers which come in a choice of pink or blue. A friend related how she loved them when she was pregnant as they were so voluminous that they pulled up right over her baby bump and were cosy and comfortable. Hen parties buy them for fun too. Nylon housecoats and button braces are still in occasional demand. Shrouds and suitcases are no longer sold.

The store was enlarged in the 1960's by taking over the neighbouring Wycherley's Pub premises. In the 1980's, the upstairs was extended to enlarge the men's department. Otherwise it is in, 2017, still almost the same store apart from reparation from the devastating flood that hit Clonakilty town and Cash's shop in June 2012. It was heart breaking for the staff to see so much stock lost and the original wooden shop counters damaged beyond repair. The clean-up job was enormous.

Today the store stocks everything from school uniforms, for both boys and girls, to every day wear and the latest European fashions for ladies. Jeans and trousers, suits and jackets galore for gents, along with all the necessary accessories like belts, ties, scarves, gloves and hats, except for shoes. Home textiles abound with cushions, rugs, pillows and small items like buttons, ribbons, pins and elastic, plus a selection of fabrics, tools and embroidery thread for creative hands. If you can't find something in the drapery line anywhere else, it is sure to be found at Cash's.

Helpful staff members are always ready to assist people in carrying things to their car. Some customers still take advantage of a service that allows them to secure an item and have it put aside, until they can complete all the payments required before they collect it.

Commercial travellers used to call in frequently in times past to take orders for stock but today they are seldom seen as modern technology takes over. Some stock is ordered twice a year, but much is ordered for delivery as the shop requires it. These items come from all over Ireland and Western Europe.

The assistants are friendly and interested and work as a well-oiled machine. Most have worked there many years and some have worked in Cash's since leaving school. Men used to serve the men, but the staff today comprises women, except for Mr Leader. Up until the late 1990's there were three competing general drapers, O'Mahoney's across the road on Rossa St, Derry McCarthy's on Asna Square and Ahern's on Connolly Street. But Cash's has outlasted them all.

With thanks to the staff for their help and memories.

All in the Cooking

Most women in this book are familiar with the secondary school textbook, "All in the Cooking". First published in 1946 it provided information on anything a student of "Domestic Economy", or housewife, would need to know from how to equip a functional kitchen, to food storage and preparation prior to cooking, along with hundreds of detailed recipes, nutrition advice and suggested menus. It offers practical advice and emphasises tasty, economical, simple to prepare dishes. The book, which was regularly updated, was in widespread use throughout Ireland until the 1970's.

In 2015 the O'Brien Press republished the book as a facsimile edition of the third edition of Book One. It is a handsome hard cover book and comes with a cute beribboned bookmark that makes sense of the quaint, old oven temperatures that cooks around the world used before ovens were equipped with thermometers. For example, a Fairly Hot Oven is described today as being 425 degrees Fahrenheit or approximately 215 degrees Centigrade, while a Very Moderate Oven is described as 350 degrees Fahrenheit. On the reverse of the bookmark are Handy Measures such as: 1 cup of Chopped meat is equivalent to 8 oz (ounces) or 227 grams.

Typical of most recipe books of the time anywhere in the world, there are no photographs, just clear descriptions and a few line drawings to show what to do. There are also eight pages of recipes relating to cooking for invalids, something seldom written about today.

The book is interesting for learning more about the making of typical Irish dishes such as Champ and Soda Bread and it will bring back many memories to those who used it in their schooldays.

Legislation Affecting Women

Year	Legislation
1918	Women have the right to vote, but only if they are over 30 and own property.
1922	All Irish women given the right to vote.
1931	Legitimacy Act: allowed re-registration of children born prior to the marriage of their parents.
1937	Irish Constitution
1952	The Register of Adopted Children introduced.
1957	Married Women's Status Act
1972	Marriage Act: increased the minimum age for marriage to 16 years [82] (High Court approval needed to marry at a lower age).
1976	Family Home Protection Act
1979	Health (Family Planning) Act
1981	Criminal Law (Rape) Act
1987	Status of Children Act: allowed the father of a child to be named on birth registration where the parents were not married to each other.
1989	Judicial Separation and Family Law Reform Act
1990	Criminal Law (Rape) (Amendment) Act
1993	Criminal Law (Sexual Offences) Act
1994	Maternity Protection Act
1995	Family Law Act
1995	Regulation of Information (Services outside the State for Termination of Pregnancies) Act
1996	Domestic Violence Act
1996	Family Law (Divorce) Act
1998	Employment Equality Act

---

[82] Formerly the ages of 12 (bride) and 14 (groom).

Other Legislation

Decimalisation of the Irish Pound (also known as Punt) was implemented in 1971, meaning that one pound equalled 100p (pence) replacing 240d (pennies).

The implementation of the official monetary unit of the Euro zone countries, of which Ireland is one, occurred on 1st January 1999, but in fact it was not until January 2002 that the state began withdrawing Irish pounds, coins and notes and replacing them with the much simpler decimal Euro where ten cents equals one tenth of a Euro etc.

Key to money prior to 1971

Farthing = ¼ of a penny
Halfpenny (Ha'penny) = ½ of a penny
Three penny coin = ¼ of a shilling
Six penny coin = ½ of a shilling
One Shilling = 12 pennies
20 Shillings = 1 pound
One Guinea = 1 pound and the same number of shillings, e.g. 5 Guineas = Five Pounds (or Punts), and 5 shillings.

Moving to the metric system for measurement of weights, lengths, volumes and speed began in the 1970's and was completed by 2005, except for the imperial pint of beer kept at 568ml by tradition.[83]

****

---

[83] Wikipedia: Metrication in Ireland

Miscellaneous Quotes

"There is a true story of a Co. Cork man who heard that his son was shot by the English in the War of Independence. He went to town to find his son. The father recognised him from a distance (by an item of clothing he wore) amongst the dead being carried away. He had to go home and say nothing to anyone, because if it became known he was related to someone who had been shot by the English, the family home would have been burned down."

"A farmer's wife was preparing to feed an influx of hungry men working on the harvest. On going to collect the cooling bread she was horrified to see the cat had made a meal of it by eating the centres out of the brown cakes. What to do? Her neighbour suggested they slice and butter the remainder and serve it so. And they did."

'When electricity came to rural Ireland most of the crossroads ghosts disappeared.'

An older neighbour was keeping turkeys. I asked her, "Does it pay to keep turkeys?" She replied, "Oh, never mind about that. It keeps the money together until Christmas".

"I wanted to set up a First Aid group and asked a priest if he would come along and give it his support. His response, 'And who will be looking after your children while you are doing this?'"

"A priest in the family is worth an outside farm."

A common Irish compliment to someone who looks younger than their age: "Well, you are looking very fresh!"

A question asked when shopping for a shirt for a man, "Does he have a meaty neck?"

An amusing anecdote told by someone who knew the people concerned:

"There once was a little old pub on a crossroads near Clonakilty. It was cosy, dark and full of character. One Sunday night around 1950 it was especially crowded with a road bowling score [84] just completed and platform dancing in full swing. The landlady was rushed off her feet. A man called for a pint and she served him. She had to reach to the very top shelf for a glass, as so many were in use. He went to drink, stopped and called her attention to the drink.

A dried-up mouse floated on the top.

"What do you want me to do with it?" she asked.

"Take it out", he replied and she did, immediately turning to the next customer.

He called her attention again.

"I don't know what is wrong with you", she said. "You were not happy with it in the drink, and now you are not happy with it out of it."

✶✶✶✶✶✶✶✶✶✶✶✶✶✶✶✶✶

---

[84] Road bowling is (mostly) male players throwing a metal ball down a rural road. The winner (on whom bets are taken) takes the fewest throws over a set distance.

Index

A

C

D

Made in the USA
Middletown, DE
16 December 2020